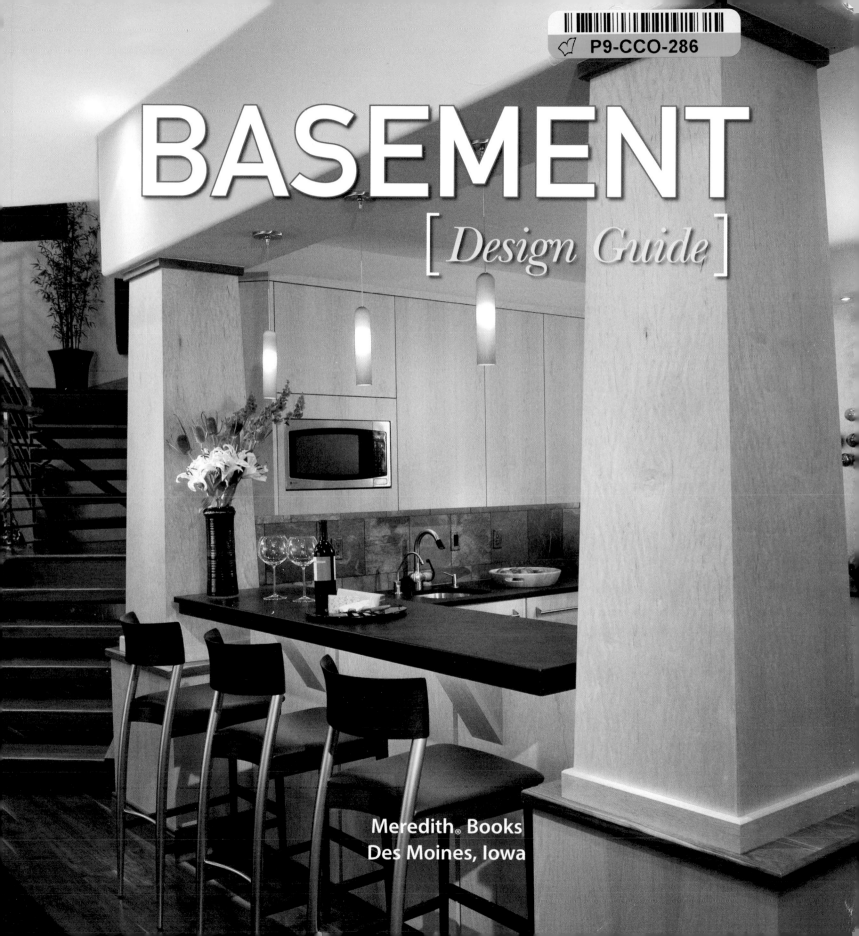

BASEMENT

[*Design Guide*]

Meredith® Books
Des Moines, Iowa

Better Homes and Gardens® *Basement Design Guide*
Editor: Vicki Christian
Contributing Editor/Writer: Lexicon Consulting, Inc.
Associate Design Director: Todd Emerson Hanson
Contributing Graphic Designer: David Jordan, Studio 22
Copy Chief: Terri Fredrickson
Copy Editor: Kevin Cox
Publishing Operations Manager: Karen Schirm
Senior Editor, Asset & Information Management: Phillip Morgan
Edit and Design Production Coordinator: Mary Lee Gavin
Editorial Assistant: Kaye Chabot
Book Production Managers: Pam Kvitne, Marjorie J. Schenkelberg,
   Rick von Holdt, Mark Weaver
Imaging Center Operator: Maggie M. Gulling
Contributing Copy Editor: Susie Fagen
Contributing Proofreaders: Tom Blackett, Michelle Pettinger, Willa Speiser
Contributing Indexer: Stephanie Reymann

Meredith® **Books**
Editor in Chief: Gregory H. Kayko
Executive Director, Design: Matt Strelecki
Managing Editor: Amy Tincher-Durik
Executive Editor: Benjamin W. Allen
Senior Editor/Group Manager: Vicki Leigh Ingham
Senior Associate Design Director: Ken Carlson
Marketing Product Manager: Brent Wiersma

Editorial Director: Linda Raglan Cunningham
Executive Director, Marketing: Kevin Kacere
Executive Director, New Business Development: Todd M. Davis
Executive Director, Sales: Ken Zagor
Director, Operations: George A. Susral
Director, Production: Douglas M. Johnston
Director, Marketing & Publicity: Amy Nichols
Business Director: Jim Leonard

Vice President and General Manager: Douglas J. Guendel

Better Homes and Gardens® **Magazine**
Editor in Chief: Gayle Goodson Butler
Deputy Editor, Home Design: Oma Blaise Ford

Meredith Publishing Group
President: Jack Griffin
Senior Vice President: Karla Jeffries

Meredith Corporation
Chairman of the Board: William T. Kerr
President and Chief Executive Officer: Stephen M. Lacy

In Memoriam: E.T. Meredith III (1933–2003)

All of us at Meredith® Books are dedicated to providing you with information and ideas to enhance your home. We welcome your comments and suggestions. Write to us at: Meredith Books, Home Decorating and Design Editorial Department, 1716 Locust St., Des Moines, IA 50309-3023.

Contents

BASEMENT
[*Design Guide*]

Finishing or remodeling your basement likely is one of the best ways to gain additional living space in your house. Whether you have some basic ideas for how to shape the lower level or you simply know that your family requires additional room and think that the basement might be the place to gain it, *Basement Design Guide* leads you through the entire process of transforming your basement into a useful, stylish living space.

Start by exploring all the possibilities for basements in Chapter 1, "Explore Your Options." If your family is feeling cramped or seems to be overflowing main-level family and living rooms, check out the practical and stylish lower-level rooms for living and entertaining, including family rooms, media rooms, entertaining zones, and kitchens. In need of extra work and play space? Look at hardworking home offices, convenient laundry rooms, fitness areas, playrooms, and creative suites conducive to pursuing your favorite hobbies and activities. Be ready when guests come to call for short or long visits by looking at fresh ideas for bedrooms, bathrooms, teen suites, and guest suites in the "Sleep & Relax" section.

After you've explored a plethora of possibilities for the basement, take the first step to making it a reality with Chapter 2, "Plan the Project." Here you'll narrow your wants and needs by working through a remodeling checklist and setting a realistic budget. Learn the ins and outs of working with professionals in design and remodeling fields, and understand what's critical when it's time to evaluate bids, estimates, and contracts.

In Chapter 3, "Evaluate Your Basement," you'll find out about a critical component of basement remodeling projects: Ensuring that the lower level is free of major problems including moisture and cracks before you begin finishing the space. An overview of typical building codes helps guarantee that the basement is ready for conversion to a comfortable living space.

Move on to Chapter 4, "Create Comfort" to find

out how to make the lower level as comfortable as possible with the right heating and cooling, plumbing, and electrical systems. Consider, too, a fireplace as both a heat source and a dramatic focal point for the new room.

Chapter 5, "Shape the Space," helps you plan the size, style, and placement of windows, doors, and stairways. And be sure not to finalize placement of interior walls until you read the tips for constructing and finishing non-load-bearing and soundproof walls.

The new basement space will come to life with the addition of a ceiling treatment, lights, and flooring. In Chapter 6, "Finish the Space," you'll see a range of options for these surface materials, along with suggestions for lighting schemes that match the function of the room. Finally, keep the clutter at bay by following handy recommendations for storage.

If you've been implementing the recommendations throughout the book, you've hit the final stages of the project when you visit Chapter 7, "Decorate the Space." Learn decorating basics and explore how color and texture enhance basement rooms. Plan finishing touches for the room after weighing options for furnishings and fabrics, window treatments, art, and accessories.

In Chapter 8, "Final Considerations," a project checklist will assist you in making sure all necessary components are included in the project. Also see how the same basement space can be configured and arranged in unique ways to best address the particular needs of three families. Use the planning kit to plot the best configuration for your basement space.

Consult Chapter 9, "Resources," for names and contact information for some of the many organizations and associations involved in residential remodeling projects. Learn the definition of helpful terms you'll use when talking with professionals about the basement project. Also refer to the professional and source listings for some of the basements featured in this book.

CHAPTER 1

Explore Your Options

Live & Entertain

Work & Play

Sleep & Relax

Planning comfortable living spaces in the basement begins with envisioning all it can become. Your basement might be a private retreat for guests, a home office and a laundry area, or even a media room. Regardless of what form your basement takes, certain elements—from the placement of walls and windows to the furnishings, lighting, and decor—that you select will help set the tone for your new living space.

To make envisioning your finished basement easier, this chapter is full of ideas for basement rooms. To guarantee that each space in your basement ultimately meets—and even exceeds—expectations, study the specific tips for planning the rooms you want to create. Well-planned details will ensure every room in your basement is as functional and comfortable as possible—whether it's for sleep, work, or play.

Live & Entertain

FAMILY ROOMS

Creating a basement family room is a smart way to increase your home's all-purpose living space. Equipped with an entertainment center, bookshelves, and comfortable furnishings, even a small basement living area draws the whole family. Be flexible. A lower-level living space can serve many functions—from relaxing with family and friends to playing board games, reading, or watching movies. Plan this area of your home well and it can be part fun zone, part entertaining space, and part theater.

Balancing major elements

Playing so many roles means your family room may be packed full of elements that can conflict with one another. You can achieve harmony by balancing these zones. A major built-in focal point in many family rooms is a fireplace. It usually dominates one wall and often dictates the arrangement of everything else. Furniture usually is positioned to take in views of the hearth.

If you sit and watch anything in the basement, however, it's probably the television, which creates another prominent point in the room. The TV is often an afterthought, stuck to one side of the fireplace because that is where it can be seen. Unfortunately neither the fireplace nor the television gets attention this way. When two elements compete, give each equal treatment. Position the firebox and television screen at the same height and use similar cabinet or wall treatments, such as in the family room, *opposite.*

For the whole family

A family room should be designed for more than watching TV or enjoying a fire. You may want bookshelves, comfortable conversation areas, and a spot for playing games. For maximum usability, fill the space with furniture such as lightweight coffee tables and modular seating pieces that are rearranged easily. Look for ottomans and benches with interior storage; built-in cabinetry or floor-to-ceiling shelving also comes in handy for storing and displaying books, movies, and family photos. Use task lighting to help define individual activity areas and allow adequate visibility.

Lighting is particularly important in living spaces where family members read or play board games. Overhead lights supply ambient illumination and a table lamp provides task lighting.

A mantel tops the big screen television and stone fireplace in this lower-level family room, artfully integrating with the built-in cabinetry. Well-placed seating and lighting make this a cozy spot.

A wallmount flat-screen television works as art here. Wires are hidden behind the wall. For easier installation, fasten the wires together in one unobtrusive line.

MEDIA ROOMS

A media room takes advantage of a basement's natural assets: darkness and separation from household activity. Plus most basements are rectangular—the shape audio-video experts recommend for rich, realistic sound.

Creating a state-of-the-art home theater involves carefully integrating a number of elements. The entertainment center and all of its related electronic parts—including the television, DVD player, and surround-sound system—are, of course, the focal point of the room. But creating a thoughtful furniture arrangement and ensuring the lighting enhances rather than detracts from the screen are important too.

Media room planning

Media rooms are all about technology, but with the right planning they can be high-tech, comfortable, stylish gathering spots. Follow these guidelines for artfully combining the television screen, seating, and sound.

Relate the screen size to seating distance. For optimum viewing, home theater installers recommend a seating distance that's 2 to 2½ times the width of a screen. For example, place the sofa and chairs 54 to 68 inches from a 27-inch screen.

The best viewing angle is usually head-on. This varies from model to model; consult the owner's manual to find out what angle is best for positioning furniture in relation to the screen.

Place primary seating at the best viewing location. Once the sofa is in place, use easily movable chairs to add seating that can be adjusted for the best view.

Stadium-Style Seating

Enhance the atmosphere in your media room with stadium-style seating that ensures everyone has a premium spot for viewing the screen.

Many furniture stores sell stadium seating, which may include such luxurious amenities as in-seat lighting, personal coolers, and cupholders. If you'd like to add stadium-style seating to the plan for a media room, take some measurements beforehand to make sure your basement can accommodate raised rows.

Calculate ceiling height. Installing stepped platforms works best in basements with 9- or 10-foot-high ceilings. An 8-foot-high ceiling may work, but if the ceiling is lower the highest platform will be too close to the ceiling to stand comfortably.

Use sturdy building materials. For a sturdy platform that will hold the weight of furniture and people, use 4×4s and 2×4s for framing, and then sheath the platform with ½-inch plywood.

Add finishing touches. Choose flooring that coordinates with the rest of the room or basement to tie the new media room to the rest of the space.

Taking a page from movie theaters, this media room includes comfortable chairs. An inset decorative filmstrip and classic movie posters further the Hollywood ambience.

Front-projection systems replicate the feel of a movie theater but require complete darkness. Rear-projection systems and picture-tube TVs produce a picture that looks good with lights on or off.

Create full surround sound with five speakers. Place one speaker on each side of the TV screen so it's level with viewers' ears when seated. Locate two speakers behind the sofa about 6 to 8 feet off the floor and at least as far apart as the front pair. Put the fifth one on top of the TV to direct dialogue. Action-movie buffs enjoy a subwoofer that intensifies the bass and those dramatic booms and bangs. Position it beneath the screen.

Stash equipment in a ventilated cabinet or on shelves so components don't overheat, avoid blocking the vents on the equipment. For easy access to the backs of audiovisual components, construct the shelving or cabinet units 4 or 5 feet in front of the basement wall to create a narrow "hallway" behind the units.

Choose dimmer light switches for optimum light control ideal for viewing.

Built-in cabinetry provides a perch for the television in this entertainment area, which includes speakers and accent lighting. When placing your electronics in built-in cabinetry, provide proper ventilation.

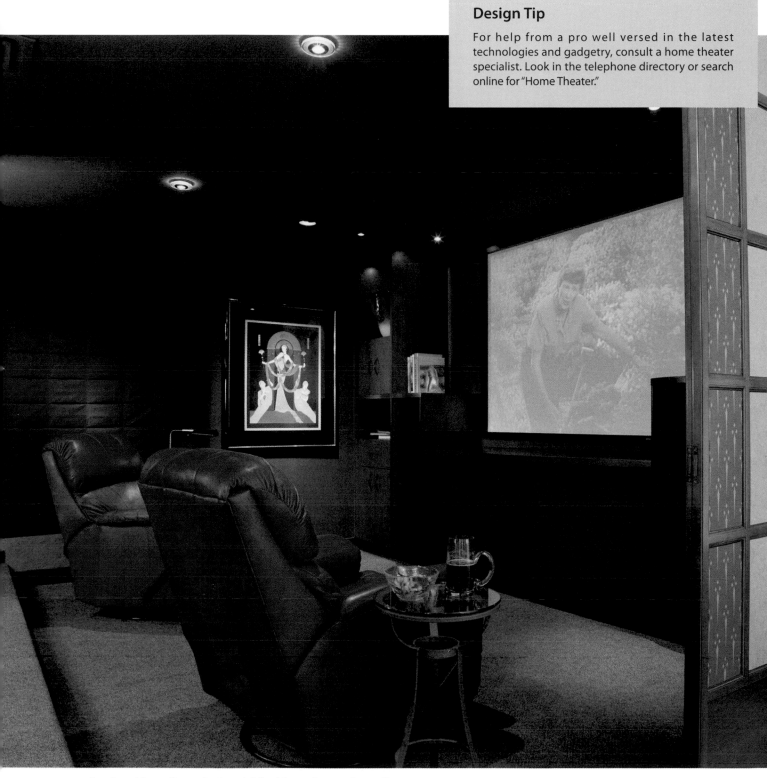

Design Tip

For help from a pro well versed in the latest technologies and gadgetry, consult a home theater specialist. Look in the telephone directory or search online for "Home Theater."

Comfortable recliners do the trick in this modest-scale media room. Small display lights over the built-ins highlight collectibles and can be dimmed during a movie for easier viewing.

Curvaceous ceiling baffles deaden the surface for better acoustics. A dropped ceiling can achieve the same effect. Install tracked halogen lamp fixtures for an affordable, custom-look lighting option.

A warm-tone wood surround makes this large television look as if it is built into the wall. Cabinets provide discreet storage below and on each side of the screen.

ENTERTAINMENT AREAS

When guests come to call, the basement can be ideal for hosting everything from intimate gatherings to full-blown celebrations. The ultimate entertaining spaces may include areas for eating and drinking, chatting with guests, playing games, and watching movies. In a walkout basement, you may wish to extend the entertaining area onto a patio or deck.

Including a built-in wet bar requires only a small alcove. A granite countertop, Douglas fir cabinetry, and stainless-steel shelf supports pack a lot of style into a tiny space.

This mini kitchen designed for throwing parties partners with an entertainment center along one wall in the basement. Situating a small kitchen along one wall maximizes cost efficiencies for running plumbing.

Focus on fun

Any entertainment area requires ample lighting and a stereo system with speakers placed strategically throughout the room. Easy-to-clean materials that withstand spills and heavy traffic are a plus.

Keep room layouts open and include distinctive activity zones. A home theater, complete with an entertainment center and comfortable seating, may occupy one corner of the room. Position a tall counter with stools or a table and chairs nearby to create a spot for playing games or snacking. A pool or table tennis table and a dartboard provide even more game night opportunities. You may choose to include a small wet bar for serving drinks or outfit part of the entertaining area with a mini kitchen that features a stretch of countertop and an undercounter refrigerator, bar sink, microwave oven, and wine cooler. For added convenience include a dishwasher so you don't have to haul dirty dishware upstairs.

Instill personality in a basement entertaining area by decorating with a theme. Perhaps it's a retro diner, complete with vinyl booths and a soda fountain. Or pay tribute to sports by displaying memorabilia from favorite athletic teams.

Comfortable furnishings, an entertainment center, and a bar ensure this basement room works for entertaining. The warm woodtones unify the open space.

Fit in a Pool Table

If you plan to include a pool table in your family room, consider the size of table and recommended clearance.

For a 7-foot bar-size pool table equipped with 48-inch-long cues, the room should be at least 11×13½ feet. For 52-inch-long cues, at least an 11½×14-foot space is necessary. If you plan to use 57-inch-long cues, the room should measure at least 12½×15 feet.

A standard 8-foot table will work in a 12×15½-foot room if you use 48-inch-long cues. If you increase cue length to 52 inches, plan a room at least 12½×16 feet. For cues measuring 57 inches long, the room should measure a minimum of 13½×17 feet.

If you're truly serious about pool, you may prefer a 9-foot tournament-size pool table. This size, coupled with 57-inch-long cues, requires a room measuring at least 14×18 feet.

For lighting, the bottom of the fixture shade should hang 31 inches above the playing surface.

In this game room a bar attached to the wall provides a spot for people to watch action on the pool table. Windows pair with lamps suspended above the table to keep the space well-lit.

KITCHENS

Basements may be designed to accommodate a fully equipped kitchen or a mini kitchen that requires fewer amenities and less space—the choice depends on needs and available space.

If you have live-in relatives or wish to rent out the basement, consider a complete kitchen with full-size appliances and upper and lower cabinetry. For most people, a wet bar or kitchenette suffices and serves daily needs as well as special-occasion parties.

Cooking basics

To create a wet bar or kitchenette, plan access to hot and cold water for a bar sink as well as electrical outlets for an undercounter refrigerator, a microwave oven, small countertop appliances, and possibly a small dishwasher or dishwasher drawer (see "Spacesaving Appliances," *below*). If you plan to include a cooktop in the basement kitchen, remember ventilation. Updraft units above the cooktop are standard. They feature a hood that collects the air and moves it through a duct, either to a filter or outside the house. Downdraft systems take the air from the cooking surface and move it down through a filter to the outside.

You'll also need to choose cabinetry and countertop materials. Stock cabinets, which come in standard sizes and styles, may do the trick for a basement kitchen if you don't want to spend much money. However, if you're looking for design flexibility or want smaller-size cabinets, you may choose custom models. Although more expensive, these cabinets often are built with better materials and provide more options for size, storage

A mini kitchen can be as much of a convenience as a full-size one. In one small slice of space, this area boasts storage, a countertop, an undercounter refrigerator, and a bar sink.

Space-saving Appliances

Many manufacturers carry smaller versions of standard appliances that may fit better in a basement kitchen.

Storing. An undercounter refrigerator as small as 2 cubic feet provides space for storing snacks and beverages. Or plan for built-in refrigerator or freezer drawers that fit 24-inch base cabinets.

Cooking. Microwave ovens—some as small as 1.4 cubic feet—take up minimal counterspace. A warming drawer is a good option to keep dishes that were prepared upstairs warm. To accommodate more cooking, look for wall ovens that fit in base cabinets or narrow wall units. Conserve surface space with cooktops or ranges that have one or two burners instead of the standard four.

Cleaning. Dishwashers come in the form of drawers to ease cleanup without taking up too much space.

An eat-in basement kitchen with a full-size refrigerator, dishwasher, and microwave makes preparing snacks easy.

options, and accessories. Likewise, an inexpensive countertop material such as laminate may suffice. Or for durability and style, install ceramic tile, natural stone, or solid-surfacing countertops instead.

At the bar

When designing a wet bar, the countertop and cabinetry help to separate the bar area from the adjoining room.

Or recess a short length of cabinetry and countertop into the family room wall with a mini refrigerator below and provide doors to close off the bar when it's not in use. For wine storage, consider a small wine refrigerator or wine racks.

A small nook behind the basement stairs is perfect for tucking in this bar area with granite countertops, a small refrigerator, a built-in wine rack, and storage for glassware.

Efficient Kitchen Layouts

Plan a smart layout to get the most out of a basement kitchen.

Kitchen layouts come in a variety of shapes and sizes. Depending on the dimensions of the kitchen and how you will use it, one or more of these basic shapes may work for your space.

One Wall. This layout is ideal when space is at a premium. Install the sink between the refrigerator and cooktop, with all three elements on one wall so the basement seems open. The downside: The design isn't the most efficient for the cook, and postmeal messes are in plain sight of the whole room.

L-Shape. Efficient for the cook and great for saving space, L-shape kitchens are another option. Install countertops on two adjacent walls and keep the work triangle focused near the corner, with the refrigerator and sink on one wall and the cooking appliance on the other.

Galley. These kitchens are built between two parallel walls, creating a compact work triangle with two elements on one side and the third placed on the opposite wall. Leave at least 4 feet between opposite counters. A peninsula or bar can be one of the sides—it can double as a casual eating area or a spot for serving drinks and will help the space appear more open.

If you have the space and the budget, a second full-scale kitchen in the basement is perfect for parties. This one includes a bar area so guests can chat with the cooks. Robust columns, light-wood cabinetry, and pendent lights add style.

DESIGN GALLERY
Media Rooms

Basements are the perfect places for creating rooms made for movie watching. And nothing frames the screen quite like an entertainment center, whether it's built-in or freestanding.

1. This custom built-in unit maximizes storage space by following the contour of the wall and tucking under the existing windows.

2. This large-scale entertainment center includes open and closed storage.

3. Corinthian columns add a classic Art Deco detail to this home theater.

4. A flat-panel television on top of a modern chest imparts contemporary style.

5. Notching out wall space for a TV and other equipment takes advantage of the area under the stairs.

Work & Play

HOME OFFICES

If you work full-time out of your home or frequently require a home office, you'll appreciate the privacy and quiet that a basement office can offer. Primary requirements for an office are light, heat, and sufficient wiring to handle telephone lines, computers, fax machines, and printers. You also may need cable or wiring to connect the computer to the Internet.

Wiring essentials

Adding stud walls provides the space to run new wiring. Because existing wiring usually is exposed in the overhead joists, it's easy to extend an electrical circuit or add a telephone jack. Adding a separate circuit to serve only the computer and other office equipment prevents drawing too much power from a single circuit, which can trip circuit breakers and cause the loss of unsaved work. Consult a licensed electrician about adding a circuit and be sure to allow for enough electrical outlets so you can move equipment around, add equipment, or change the layout of your office later.

Light and comfort

Proper lighting is particularly important for an office area. Include soft, diffuse light that illuminates the whole

Building codes require that windows with wells deeper than 44 inches be fitted with steps or a ladder. This approach cleverly transforms the steps into perches for potted plants, creating a gardenlike view outside a basement office.

Design Tip

Make your home office comfortable and organized, because you may spend a lot of time there. Treat yourself to a palette of your favorite colors and include amenities that ease tasks, such as a copier, a conference table, and plenty of storage for files and supplies. The office can pull double duty as a retreat for overnight guests if you include a sofa sleeper.

This diminutive home office packs a lot into a small space thanks to a slim corner-unit desk. Tiered shelves provide spots for all the necessities within a compact footprint.

Designed to flow seamlessly from the home's light-filled living spaces, this work area has warmth and personality. The workstation's efficient U-shape and an expansive wall of storage ensure there's plenty of room for everything a home office requires.

room as well as desk and floor lamps that direct light where you need it most.

If the basement is especially humid, be sure to install a portable dehumidifier to protect books, documents, and sensitive electronics. Basement floors are usually cool in all seasons, so also consider an insulated floor to prevent feet and legs from becoming chilled if you'll be sitting at the desk for extended periods of time.

Include plenty of shelves, drawers, and other storage for supplies, papers, books, and magazines. In addition to a desk with an open work surface, consider a separate table and chairs in one corner of the office to provide extra workspace and serve as a conference area.

Locating your home office near the basement wet bar can provide a convenient location for making coffee as well as offer access to the refrigerator for soft drinks and snacks.

Professional Welcome

A home office that's easily accessible, inviting, and professional reflects well on you and your business. If clients regularly visit your home office, consider what you'll need to include to make the space welcoming and professional.

A separate entrance is ideal. The office should be readily accessible from the outside, and clients should easily recognize it as a business entrance. For example, a basement room with an exterior door facing the street would be easy for visitors to spot. After checking local zoning ordinances, add an exterior sign with your business name and logo near the door for extra clarity.

Interior details can go a long way in making clients feel comfortable. Be sure to have a place to hang coats and hats, and consider creating a waiting area with chairs and a table. Depending on your business needs, you may decide to include a conference table with several chairs or one or two chairs near your desk. Consider locating a bathroom near your office if you anticipate long meetings, so clients won't have to wander through your home.

Clean and organize your office frequently. Haphazard paperwork or a jumble of toys immediately lowers the level of professionalism. The same concept applies to the exterior appearance of your office. Keep walkways clear, landscaping trimmed and healthy, and stairways and railings clean. Maintenance costs for repairing and cleaning your home office may be tax-deductible business expenses. Check with an accountant or tax adviser before claiming home office tax deductions.

Work & Play

LAUNDRY AREAS

Keep the inevitable tangle of clothes and noise from disrupting the rest of your home by creating a well-equipped laundry room in the basement. Besides the washer and dryer, an efficient lower-level laundry room includes moisture-proof surfaces, plenty of storage, bins for sorting laundry, and space for ironing clothes.

A wall adjacent to the washer and dryer in this laundry room includes a sink, a long countertop, and plenty of white-painted cabinets for storage.

Laundry's Latest

Before you begin shopping for a new washer and dryer, check out some of the latest features laundry appliances offer.

Conservation. Why conserve one valuable resource when you can conserve them all? Many of today's laundry appliances are designed to conserve space, water, and energy. Front-load designs are compact yet offer a large load capacity. And they often use half the water of a traditional top-loading washer and less electricity than a standard dryer.

Steam Clean. Steam washers reduce water and electricity use while killing germs with blasts of hot steam. Even dry-clean-only clothes can benefit from a quick steam cycle, which rids fabrics of odors and creases without a full wash.

Dependable Drying. Certain washers spin so fast that clothes come out of the washer almost dry. Many dryers now have the capability to dry laundry to the precise moisture level you choose. Sensors monitor clothing during the dry cycles and display the dryness level so you know when the load is almost done.

Little Upgrades. If you enjoy extra features, look for additions such as a sloped-front cabinet for easy loading and unloading, automatic bleach and fabric softener dispensers, and touch-screen controls. All are added benefits that take some of the hassle out of doing laundry.

All in the details

Typical laundry hookups include hot and cold water supply lines and a drainage system—items readily accessible in a basement. Gas dryers need access to gas lines. Electric and gas dryers require venting to the outside. You may wish to add a floor drain to handle any spills or overflows from a malfunctioning washing machine.

In small spaces consider a stacked washer and dryer, which will fit into a closet-size area. A fold-down ironing board is another spacesaver. For added convenience, include a laundry chute. A countertop makes it easy to fold clothes on the spot, and a rod or rack near the dryer and ironing board provide a place to hang clothing fresh from the dryer.

This laundry room offers ample counterspace for folding clothes. The cabinetry colors coordinate with one of the hues in the backsplash, creating a room that's as stylish as it is functional.

Laundry Hideaway

If your transformed basement displaces a sprawling, baskets-everywhere laundry room, resolve the issue with a laundry-in-a-closet. This compact solution fits in a 6×3-foot slice of space—or less if you opt for a stacked washer and dryer. Aside from ensuring you select the appropriate size appliances, consider:

Access to utilities, specifically hot and cold water supply lines, a drainage system, and electrical outlets.

An exterior wall location so the clothes dryer can be vented to the outdoors.

A floor drain to help control overflows and leaks. To accommodate for the required amount of downslope for the drainpipe, you may need to place the appliances on a platform.

Additional amenities make doing laundry even easier. Include a 4-foot fluorescent lighting fixture and a shelf to hold detergent, dryer sheets, and other laundry necessities. If there's room, include a bar for hanging clothes.

Consulting a professional or local building code official for assistance with electrical or plumbing work.

Cubbies replace standard wire shelving for a space-smart, attractive look above this washer and dryer tucked in a closet. Baskets and glass canisters store supplies with style.

Raised front-load washers and dryers with large doors make doing laundry easier. A counter over the front-loading appliances creates space for folding clothes. Wire baskets provide nearby storage.

FITNESS ROOMS

If you've ever allowed a treadmill to languish in an out-of-the-way corner of the house, consider creating a space in your basement designed especially for exercise. People are more likely to regularly use a well-designed fitness room outfitted with quality equipment. Converting basement space into an exercise room is relatively easy because little, if any, plumbing or extra electrical work is required.

Plan the exercise room on paper first. You may wish to leave open floor space for doing yoga or stretching after a workout. Provide a minimum of 30 inches between pieces of exercise equipment.

Design Tip

Think safety when planning and using a basement fitness room. Floor-to-ceiling mirrors allow weightlifters to watch their form, control their posture, and avoid injury. When you're using heavy free weights, enlist the help of a spotter. Electric fitness equipment such as treadmills should have safety keys or switches to prevent children from turning them on without adult supervision. Finally, don't forget to stow workout gear after you finish.

Workout style

Create a workout environment suited to your style, whether it's quiet and meditative or energizing with sights and sounds. If you're adding 2×4 walls, remember to run the wires and cable for stereo and television before covering the studs with drywall. Fixing a television to a swiveling, ceiling-mount bracket or creating a built-in niche in the wall allows you to view the television from anywhere in the room. Include a VCR or DVD player to view exercise videos.

Install tough, durable flooring—vinyl, rubber, or cork tiles are appropriate choices. If you prefer carpet, select a tightly woven style that cushions your step without cramping your routine. Create the illusion of a larger space with a floor-to-ceiling mirror, which also helps you observe your exercising form and technique.

A treadmill, free weights, and a ceiling-mount television transform an otherwise empty corner into a fitness area adjacent to a finished guest suite.

Family time and fitness combine in a room with seating,
a treadmill, a wall of mirrors, and a wild and wavy
climbing wall.

CREATIVE SUITES

Away from the core of household activity, basements make great locations for a specially equipped space for exploring creative interests. You'll marvel at the inspiration and productivity that come from having a place dedicated to your work or your hobbies and a place where your supplies and tools are close at hand. If your hobby is noisy, others may appreciate that you have your own space too.

Start by estimating how much space your hobby requires. Some hobby rooms call for a specialized shape or more square footage than others. Feeding an 8-foot board through woodworking machinery may dictate having workspace at least 16 feet long—much larger than a quilting studio might require, for example. Working with awkwardly shaped materials, such as sheets of plywood, may require a workspace with ceilings higher than the conventional 8 feet. Hobbies such as modeling or electronics, however, typically call for little more than a desk-size space.

Customize conveniences

One advantage of a dedicated hobby room over a dual-purpose space is the ability to add customized conveniences. Install a utility sink for cleanup and a ready water source. Wire in 220-volt outlets and electrical breakers to accommodate commercial-quality tools.

Some hobbies are noisier and messier than others, so consider how your hobby space will relate to the rest of the house. Additional soundproofing and solid-core doors for a music room, for example, will help keep practice sessions muted from the rest of the household.

To organize supplies, consider a wall of modular shelves, drawers, and cabinets. You can find your supplies at a glance in see-through bins. Include a generous-size worktable and comfortable stools, and make sure your work area is well lit. If you enjoy painting or drawing, you may want illumination that mimics natural light, such as halogen task lighting. By contrast, a woodworking shop benefits from an abundance of bright, fluorescent light fixtures.

A hobby room's decor also can be influenced by your hobby, so install display spaces to show off your projects. After all, a hobby room should not only allow for accomplishments, it should inspire them.

Creative Comfort

Regardless of the hobby or interest you're undertaking, creating a comfortable work area in your basement ensures you'll want to spend plenty of time there.

Prevent muscle fatigue that comes from standing on hard surfaces by placing soft nonstick rubber mats on the floor where you'll be working. If you don't like the look of the mats, cover them with decorative rugs.

Avoid overloading electrical circuits by dedicating circuits to individual pieces of equipment. Route the circuits through a subpanel with a master switch that allows you to turn off power to all equipment when the room is not in use.

Soundproof your workshop if your work (such as woodworking or playing a musical instrument) is noisy or requires peace and quiet. If you are finishing your basement, choose densely packed insulation—the tighter it's packed, the more soundproof it will be. For basements that are finished, manufactured soundproof wall coverings can be purchased in panels or rolls and hung directly on the drywall. Look for them at home improvement centers.

Install a fan and at least two operable windows for ventilation and to direct exhaust fumes out of the house if you are working with wood, painting, or doing anything else that might require fresh air.

Although this storage-packed studio was designed for a potter, it could be adapted for sewing or painting by switching the potter's wheel for a center worktable. A hammered-copper sink handles cleanup, and the floor benefits from the protection of vinyl-coated grass matting and a floorcloth.

PLAYROOMS

Provide a spot for children to play, teenagers to hang out, or the whole family to gather with a basement play space. As with many of the other options explored in this chapter, elements of playrooms are easy to integrate with other functional spaces, such as family rooms, entertaining areas, or creative spaces.

Just for Kids

A children's playroom might include a spot for playing with blocks, dolls, and other toys on the floor; a corner filled with items for dress-up; and a kid-size table for crafts projects. For older children, include comfortable seating, a television and game station, and a desk or table for doing homework. If your kids are old enough, let them have a hand in selecting color for walls, furnishings, and decor. Infusing the space to match their tastes is one way to ensure kids will spend time there. When creating a special area for children's play, also consider these suggestions.

Safety. Make sure the play area features an egress window or other exit.

Materials. Choose durable, easy-to-clean wall and floor treatments. If children sprawl on the floor to play, consider carpeting or rugs.

Fun. Mount a big mirror securely on the wall; children love to play in front of mirrors. Paint one wall with chalkboard paint so the kids can write and draw on the wall with chalk, or install an erasable marker board.

Cleanup. Kids will be more likely to pick up their toys if you provide see-through storage solutions. Shelves, stacking bins, and hooks make finding a child's favorite things and remembering what goes where easier.

Inspiration. Stimulate play with high-contrast color schemes. Black and white or vibrant, opposing colors are energizing.

A child-size table and chairs, chalkboard easel, and rocking horse make one corner of a basement room kid friendly. Walkout basements such as this one mean children can easily take playtime outside on nice days. Easy-to-clean flooring such as vinyl or laminate helps to eliminate messes from muddy shoes or spills.

Ample space within a colonnade area in this basement accommodates a pool table; more game space is to the left. Track lighting zeroes in on the pool table.

Kid-Friendly Organization

It's all fun and games until the playroom turns into a disaster zone. Try these storage and organization solutions.

Choose open, accessible storage. Keep simple baskets at a low level so kids easily can put away their toys. Use an open bookshelf rather than a cabinet with several doors and drawers.

Ditch the toy bin. Throwing every toy into one big bin will result in kids dumping out the entire bin when it's playtime—plus, toy bins with heavy lids can be dangerous. Instead, designate smaller baskets or bins for different types of toys: one for dolls, one for games, one for books, and so on. That way toys are easier to find and the room will stay more organized.

Think vertically. Use a tall shelf unit to organize games by how often they're played. Put favorites near the bottom so kids can reach them, and reserve top shelves for games that only get played on special occasions.

Conceal clutter. Outfit a plain bookshelf with simple curtains. Leave them open when it's playtime, and pull them shut when you want a quick fix for hiding clutter.

Take inventory. It's hard to believe how many toys, books, and games kids accumulate. The more they have, the harder it is to keep organized. A couple of times a year, weed out toys your children have outgrown and donate them to charity.

WINE CELLARS

The inherently cool climate of the basement makes it a natural place to store wines. The best wine cellars duplicate natural conditions found in underground caves in France and Italy where winemakers have been storing wine for hundreds of years.

To maintain the suggested 50- to 58-degree temperature range, however, you'll probably need a cooling system and insulation in the walls and ceiling, as well as a polyethylene vapor barrier. You can build and insulate a room from scratch, or check with a number of companies that offer kits for creating a cooled, walk-in room. To keep the conditioned air in and warm air out, install 2×4 walls with rigid foam insulation and vapor barriers on both sides. The door should be insulated and weather-sealed.

Other options

If you don't want to dedicate an entire room to wine storage, you can finish a closet-size space or custom-fit a manufactured wine cooler. Refrigerator-type wine cooling units are available in a variety of sizes and styles.

Whether you have a full-size wine cellar, an undercounter cooler, or a stash of wine bottles in a standard rack, create a wine-tasting space in your basement by adding a table and chairs or bar area and stools. That way you'll have an inviting spot for hosting wine tastings with friends or simply relaxing with a nice bottle of Merlot.

Be a Wine Connoisseur

If you build a basement wine cellar, remember to:

Keep wines cool and dry. Wines last longer when stored at temperatures between 50°F and 58°F. To keep white wine cooler than red, store whites on the bottom racks and the reds on top, because cold air naturally settles at floor level. Keep humidity levels low with a dehumidifier.

Rack 'em up. Most wine bottles should be stored on their sides in racks—purchased or custom-made—so the cork won't dry out. Make sure the racks are good quality and strong enough to hold the bottles, which can weigh up to 3 pounds each.

Stay organized. Store bottles on racks according to the types of wines to make it easy to find the one you want.

Floor-to-ceiling racks in this walk-in wine room allow storage of a large number of bottles in a relatively small space. The arched window opens to access a ledge where a bartender can serve beverages during parties.

An expansive walk-in wine cellar stores hundreds of bottles. A countertop and lighting allow for wine tastings right in the cellar.

DESIGN GALLERY
Desks

Whether your basement desk area is made for work or fun, look for ways to integrate functionality and style. With the right setup you'll want to spend time at your desk—regardless of the task at hand.

1. A family room office provides a spot for paying bills.

2. A simple, sleek desk fits discreetly along one wall in a basement family room.

3. Pretty patterns and plenty of storage define this corner office and sewing center.

4. In this crafts room a long countertop provides space for projects; a sink makes cleanup easy.

5. Funky colors help make this office fun.

6. An armoire fitted with shelves and a slide-out keyboard tray looks like a wardrobe when its doors are closed.

3

5

6

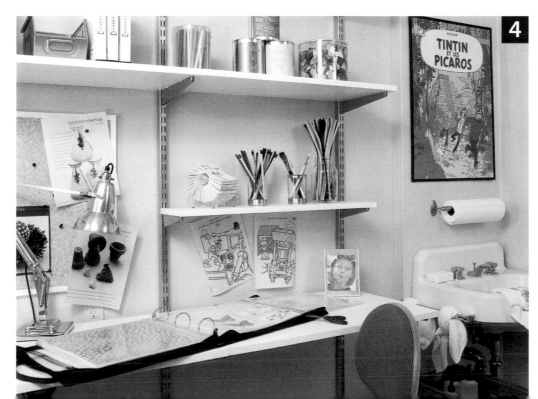

4

TINTIN
ET LES
PICAROS

BEDROOMS

Naturally cool and quiet, a basement bedroom can be one of the most inviting retreats in the house for you, other family members, or guests. As you plan, consider who will sleep in the basement and what you'd like to include in the bedroom to determine the best dimensions for your needs. To comfortably fit a double bed, plan for a room with a minimum of 125 square feet. A room at least 150 square feet fits two twin beds.

Codes usually require a wallmount light switch immediately inside the door. Direct access to the outside—an egress—also is necessary in case of fire or other emergency. If your basement is not a walkout, plan for an egress window or door. (Learn more about egresses on page 124.)

Be sure to install a smoke alarm outside the bedroom door and another over the stairway. A carbon monoxide alarm is also an important addition.

Consider comfort

In the bedroom, carpeting provides warmth and comfort underfoot. Quiet the sound of footsteps overhead by placing fiberglass insulation between joists in the ceiling. Consider shrubbery or a fence in front of windows to enhance privacy.

Locate a bathroom near—or even adjoining—the bedroom as an added convenience for overnight guests. Be sure to include storage for linens as well as for any toiletries, cleaning products, and other necessities.

If you're short on space in the basement, consider furnishing a guest bedroom that serves multiple functions. For example, include an armoire that opens to reveal a home office. Or place a treadmill and weight bench in one corner so the space doubles as a workout room when guests aren't around.

French doors allowing ample sunlight and access to outdoor spaces prevent a basement bedroom from feeling dark and damp.

Long-term guests appreciate the thoughtful amenities in this guest room. Bedside tables hold reading material and task lighting. Simple storage allows guests to stow belongings and stay organized.

Design Tip

Before selecting a mattress consider who will use the bed and for how long. For occasional overnight guests, an inexpensive yet comfortable mattress should suffice. If a family member will use the bed as primary sleeping space, choose the mattress as if it's your own bed. Test a variety of mattresses before making a final selection.

Welcoming decor—including beautiful bedding, artwork, and ample lighting—creates a inviting lower-level bedroom.

BATHROOMS

Including a bathroom in your basement-finishing plans is sure to increase the value of your home and promises convenience for you, your family, and guests. Before you begin selecting materials and fixtures, think about how you plan to use your basement as a whole. This may affect the size and layout of your bath. For instance, if your plan includes a basement fitness room, you'll probably want to fit a shower into the bathroom even if it's a small space. If you're including the bath as part of a guest suite, you may wish to include some bathroom storage and perhaps a tub-shower combination. For a basement that's all about entertaining, perhaps all you need is a powder room.

Plan for plumbing

Adding a bathroom to the basement isn't much different from fitting one in on the main level; the closer you can locate the bathroom to the main drain line, however, the easier the installation for a shower and toilet.

The job may require cutting and removing concrete to splice into the existing drain line. One solution is to elevate the new bathroom—if you have the headroom available—to create underfoot space in which to conceal new plumbing lines and a drain.

If you are building a new house and are considering an additional bathroom in the basement for some time in the future, be sure your builder understands your plans and roughs in necessary plumbing at the proper locations. It's much easier and less expensive to provide for your future plumbing needs now than to add them after concrete floors are poured and the foundation walls are constructed.

Materials and fixtures

Just as in upstairs bathrooms, you'll want to select materials with your bath's functionality and style in mind. If you're building a bath on a budget, laminate or vinyl flooring is probably the best option. Or consider ceramic or stone tiles, which cost a little more but are common options because they're durable, water-resistant, and easy to clean.

Laminate is typically the most affordably priced and widely used material for countertops too, although other possibilities include hard-wearing, low-maintenance solid-surfacing and dramatic, durable ceramic tile. Stone tiles, natural stones, and even glass are other countertop options.

When it comes to bathroom fixtures, perhaps the most important consideration is how much space is available and how you want to use it. If you're opting for a simple powder room, all you need is a pedestal sink and a toilet. For a luxurious guest suite, you may want a compartmentalized bath with separate areas for double sinks, the toilet, and the tub-shower combination. Use illustrations on page 52 to determine how much space you'll need for fixtures.

Satisfy a Small Space

With careful planning even a tiny bath can boast major style. Here are three ways to make the most of your basement bath.

Look up. Sometimes a physical expansion is out of the question. Redirect the focus from the close quarters by moving the eye up. Emphasize the room's height with tile, a wallpaper border, or interesting ceiling treatments.

Borrow from a neighbor. Echo an adjacent room's color scheme. A small space benefits when it shares colors and styles with nearby rooms. A continuous flow makes both rooms seem larger.

Create a focus. Every bathroom needs a focal point. A busy space, however, can overwhelm and distract, so stick to one or two signature pieces. Whether it's an exotic mirror, sophisticated tiling, or a decorative tub, a focal point adds distinguished flair.

The contemporary-style vanity with an undermounted sink and limestone countertop steals the show in this bathroom. The room's pale hues and the natural light filtered through the glass-block window make the small space seem bigger than it is.

An integrated tub and shower clad in travertine tile work in tandem in this basement bath. The window in the shower is high enough to provide privacy while allowing for ventilation and light.

Lighting

Light is important anywhere in a basement space but particularly so in the bath. Proper bath lighting should provide shadowless, glare-free illumination throughout the room. In addition to ambient or general lighting, you'll want to include task lighting to eliminate shadows where you perform specific tasks such as applying makeup, shaving, or taking a bath.

Because the bathroom mirror serves as a primary grooming center, make sure light is evenly distributed from above, below, and on both sides of the mirror. No matter your approach to mirror lighting, always select bulbs that are designed for vanity illumination: These bulbs create light in the daylight spectrum range. Avoid choosing bulbs that are too white or too yellow in color, or the mirror won't reflect a true picture of how you look outside the bathroom.

In an enclosed shower or tub area, place the light fixtures so they fully illuminate the tub or shower but don't shine directly in your eyes. For safety purposes, shower fixtures always should be waterproof and steamproof. All light switches should be at least 6 feet from a tub or shower.

Nightlights make late-night or early-morning trips to the bathroom more comfortable for people of all ages. For an easy, affordable solution, plug in an automatic nightlight that senses the amount of light coming into the room. Or install a low-voltage system below the vanity toe-kick or around some shelving to provide soft illumination anytime.

For more information on lighting your basement, see pages 144–147.

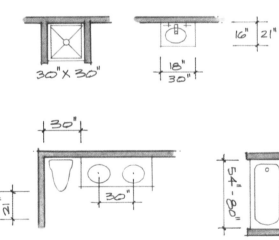

These illustrations show how much space is needed for bath fixtures and the clearance to use them comfortably. Bathroom fixtures come in a variety of shapes and sizes, so if you have an odd-shape space you probably can find a fixture to fit it.

Proving that universal design can be as beautiful as it is practical, this stunning marble-lined basement bath features a shower free of doors or a raised threshold, making it easily accessible.

Design Tip

Without proper ventilation, the humid conditions in a bathroom can lead to mold and mildew. When computing ventilation requirements for a basement bath, consider the size of the room and the number and placement of windows. Basement bathrooms are well served by a ventilation fan that moves air from the bath to the outdoors. In fact, many local building codes require exhaust fans.

This lower-level powder room boasts a vessel sink, bold tile backsplash, and pendent lights.

This small basement bath includes all of the amenities guests need, including a spacious shower with a handheld sprayer and plenty of towel storage.

A curved-front sink and walk-in shower are two luxury features in this lower-level bath. Rough-hewn stone tiles in a variety of shapes and sizes add visual interest to the space.

Universal Design for Your Bath

Tubs, showers, and other bathroom elements pose safety hazards for people of all ages. Use the following checklist—culled from basic principles of universal design—to ensure that your basement bathroom is safe and easy to use for everyone, now and for years to come.

Widen doorways to a minimum of 32 inches—36 inches is better.

Use lever handles, which are easier to grasp than knobs, on doors.

Select slip-proof floors and eliminate changes in elevation.

Install grab bars at toilets, showers, and tubs.

Install seating areas in tubs and showers.

Include detachable, handheld sprayers for rinsing off in tubs and showers.

Place faucets toward the front of the sink for easy reach.

Use lever faucet controls rather than knobs.

Install antiscald faucet devices.

TEEN SUITES

A basement is the perfect spot to provide privacy for teens who want independence and plenty of space to call their own. A teen suite may be as simple as a bedroom

and bathroom in the basement—perhaps in the vicinity of a living room so your child isn't isolated from family life. If there's space the suite also may include additional areas for your teen to study or entertain friends.

Having their own basement suite allows teens the opportunity to infuse their living spaces with personality. They might choose to paint the walls bold colors, arrange funky furniture, or include other personal touches. When designing the suite, you'll probably want to create a space that works for your teen now but can transition to a guest suite once he or she has moved out.

Safe, warm, and bright

Safety is paramount in the basement if people are living there long-term. Make certain to include at least one window that can serve as an emergency exit. Be sure that each room includes a fire alarm and carbon monoxide detector as well. Lighting and comfort are critical too—your child won't want to spend any time in his or her room if it's dark and damp, so be certain to select proper lighting, suitable flooring materials, and an efficient heating system so the suite feels comfortable, not subterranean. Learn more about all of these elements in Chapters 4 through 6.

The bedroom area of this teen suite boasts color and contemporary style, but it's classic enough to easily transition to a guest suite. A running shelf displays favorite items, and a sliding glass partition separates the bedroom from an adjoining sitting area.

The sitting area continues the same color scheme and decorating style shown in the bedroom, *opposite*. The sofa converts to another bed for guests. Windows allow natural light and provide a safe route for exiting in case of emergency.

GUEST SUITES

Whether it's made for visitors in town for a weekend, a grown child living at home for a while, or an older parent who's staying long-term, a basement guest suite provides a way to offer a private, comfortable living space for guests right in your own home. To create a suite that welcomes guests for one night or many, consider the amenities you require in your own room. A combination of good lighting, inviting materials, and comfortable temperatures will make anyone feel at home.

Basements tend to stay cool in the summer, so air-conditioning may not be needed. However, you may want an additional heat source to keep a bedroom or bathroom

Welcoming Details

Use these small, thoughtful touches to help visitors feel at home in your guest suite.

Set out extra blankets in case guests get chilly.

Keep a pitcher or bottles of water near the bed and put a few of your guest's favorite snacks in a basket.

Place a few books and magazines in the room and consider adding a small television if there's space.

Create space for a writing desk with stationery and pens for guests who need to get work done or want to keep in touch with friends and family.

Make sure there's plenty of light in the room and that lamps are placed in convenient locations—particularly on the desk and near the bed.

Stock the bathroom with fluffy towels. Small bottles of shampoos, conditioners, and lotions and travel-size toothpaste tubes add convenience.

cozy. In-floor radiant heating, which is discussed on page 152, is one solution. In addition, include at least one window that can serve as an emergency exit as well as fire alarms and carbon monoxide detectors for safety.

All about ease

A comfortable bed in a quiet room is a top requirement for a good night's sleep. Good lighting and subdued decor are important too, so your guests feel welcome in their private quarters. Aside from an inviting bedroom and functional bathroom (preferably with direct access between the two), consider what other elements will make your guests comfortable.

A sitting area or living space provides a spot for guests to unwind; include an office with an Internet connection so they can catch up with email or correspondence.

A surround of cabinetry provides plenty of storage for guests in this cozy suite. Windows above the cabinets and the mirror above the bed help the small space appear larger and brighter. The adjacent bath offers privacy and convenience.

Similar neutral tones throughout the bath and adjacent bedroom make this small suite seem larger. This neutral decorating scheme also helps the guest suite function best since the style of the space is comfortable for everyone.

If space is at a premium, at least try to design a bedroom large enough to accommodate a desk, television, and other basic amenities. If possible, include a mini kitchen or breakfast bar area stocked with food and beverages. That way if guests want an early-morning or late-night snack they don't have to feel as if they are intruding upstairs.

Storage is also important in a guest suite. If visitors will only be staying for a short time, a closet and luggage rack in the bedroom and some undercounter storage in the bath may suffice. To accommodate long-term guests, try to include as much storage as possible so they can put their belongings away and feel settled. Consider including a dresser or two in the bedroom, additional cabinetry or shelving in the bath, and even some portable storage—perhaps in the form of wicker baskets—scattered throughout the living spaces.

This comfortably-appointed suite is designed to serve as a long-term living space for the homeowner's mother. The bedroom area, *opposite*, includes decor that reflect the occupant's love for Old-World art, antiques, and furnishings. A hallway between the bedroom and the private bath, *above*, serves as a dressing area with closets on each side.

Accessible Living

Principles of universal design—a general concept that makes a home more livable for people of all ages, but particularly the disabled or elderly—can make your basement a more comfortable space for any guests. Flexibility and easy access are the cornerstones of universal design. In general keep in mind how someone who uses a wheelchair or has arthritis will be able to comfortably use the basement space. Consider the following concepts when planning:

Create wider doorways to accommodate wheelchairs; 36-inch doorways are ideal.

Plan for threshold-free, step-free entries and bump-free transitions between flooring materials to avoid tripping hazards and accommodate those using a wheelchair.

Allow 4-foot passageways from one space to the next and 5-foot approach space near activity areas and beds. These dimensions will provide room to maneuver wheelchairs.

Make sure there are 36 inches clear on two sides of the bed, and 60 inches on the third side.

Create an uninterrupted path—no rugs, wires, or furniture—from the bed to the bathroom and doorway.

Consider the placement of handles, switches, outlets, and appliances. Place all these items 15 to 48 inches above the floor, which is within comfortable reach for most people.

Outfit storage cabinets with roll-out drawers so contents can be pulled into view.

DESIGN GALLERY
Bathrooms

Most people include a bathroom in their basement plans. Whether it's a powder room for occasional use or a full-size bath designed for long-term guests, nothing is as important as comfort and convenience.

1

2

1. Exterior windows and wall sconces illuminate this vanity area.

2. Glass-block windows usher light and provide privacy in a luxurious bath with a spacious walk-in shower.

3. Bright and cheerful, this guest suite provides touches to make visitors feel at home.

4. Powder rooms require minimal space and usually include only a toilet and sink.

5. Mosaic tiles often come on backing, allowing placement of several tiles at once.

CHAPTER 2

Plan the Project

Determining Needs, Floor Plans, Budgets, Professionals, Bids,
Estimates & Contracts, DIY Considerations

Now that your mind is filled with basement design ideas, identify what you need in your own basement—and what's required to get it to that point. Look at what the remodeling process involves from start to finish. Then determine your needs—and throw in a few items from your wish list for good measure. After you've drafted a floor plan, estimate the costs and decide who will do the work. Consider having your ideas reviewed by design professionals, and look at the services they offer to see how they can refine and improve your basement rooms. If you plan to hire a contractor, use the advice in this chapter to obtain bids and sort through the estimates. As you'll learn here, all of this preliminary work is your ticket to discovering how much you can enjoy the remodeling journey that will take you to your finished basement.

PLAN WITH A PURPOSE

The task of remodeling your basement might seem overwhelming, but the undertaking is much less so when it's broken down into smaller steps. Take a look at this progression of work, and then keep this plan and the remodeling checklist on pages 70–71 handy as a guide throughout the project.

Collect ideas

Get a sense of what others have done with their basements. You already started this phase in the first chapter of this book, but don't stop there. Flip through magazines, books, and brochures for ideas. Start a clipping folder of articles and photographs that show ideas and design details that appeal to you. Mark clippings so you remember what you liked about them—maybe a layout, a surface material, or a decorative technique. Jot down notes about how you want to finish the space and your ideas for using it. Devote at least a month to this phase; some people spend a year or two gathering ideas. If you do spend that much time, you will have a good sense of what you like and be prepared when it's time to begin the project.

Gather facts

The time to get a feel for your basement transformation potential is before your need for space begins to cramp your living style. Study your available space and identify your current and future needs. Local real estate appraisers can help you get a feel for improvements that are appropriate for your neighborhood. "Learn Building Code Requirements" on pages 102–103 can help you learn about visiting your city's building department to discuss space and needs in broad terms and find out what's possible and what's not.

At this point you'll also want to determine whether your space is weathertight or, if not, how to take the steps to make it so. See "Solve Major Problems" beginning on page 94 for more details. Many homeowners weatherproof their unfinished basements and test them through a few seasons to be confident they're ready to remodel when the time comes. There's no time like the present to work through the section "Bids, Estimates,

and Contracts" on pages 85–87; it helps bring your needs and wants into focus.

Check out materials

Shopping for materials before you fine-tune your plans may seem premature, but what you choose—in terms of both construction method and surface materials—has an effect on your final direction. So collect those ideas and drop them in your binder. Spend

Even if your current needs don't call for an additional bathroom, it makes sense to rough in the plumbing now if you might want one in the future.

Painting the walls and installing decorative trimwork, such as this wood wainscoting, fall near the end of the remodeling process.

some time thinking about what you plan to use before you move on to the next stage.

Move toward the details

Rough plans must be solidified in order to implement them. Figure out every detail, from storage and utilities to finishing methods and decorative trims. The following chapters will help you get to this point. If you go this far

Design Tip

Control costs by finalizing plans before work begins. One of the biggest budget-blowers is changing your plans. Modifying the placement of a wall on paper may result in minimal charges if you've hired a design professional to draw your plans. Changing the placement of a wall once construction has begun may be a major expense.

designing the basement spaces on your own, enlist an architect or a building designer to review your plans. They can spare you the trouble and expense of oversights later. Give yourself a couple of months in this phase.

Hone your choices

This step can be difficult, but eliminating details or amenities that won't fit your budget or time frame must be done. Gathering ideas can be easy, but separating them into wants versus must-haves is more difficult. Don't despair! For example, hang on to that great wet bar idea that you can't work into the budget today. Perhaps you can run the plumbing lines now and install the cabinets, sink and faucet, countertop, and wine chiller in the future.

Decide who will do the work

Perhaps you want to do the remodeling work, or maybe you'd rather hire it out. Now is the time to give the topic serious consideration. Track down your general contractor or subcontractors and prepare your space for transformation. This chapter will walk you through these decisions. Allow two months for this stage.

Prepare for the actual work

If you're doing the work, it's time to apply for building permits and prepare a calendar of work, material-ordering dates, and inspections that will take place along the way. Building permits are good only for a certain amount of time; discuss scheduling—plus inspections—with your city's building department. It's also time to prepare the rest of your home for the remodeling effort: Relocate activities, reroute entries, protect traffic routes through the house, and arrange for large trash receptacles, if necessary. A couple of weeks, if that, is all you need for this effort.

Order materials

You'll need to order materials several times throughout the project, arranging for them to arrive when you need them. If you have ample storage space available—such as in the garage—you can order items even further ahead. Keep in mind, however, that plans could change (such as discovering an unforeseen structural obstacle) that might make some items unusable and often unreturnable.

Get started

It's time to strap on a tool belt and start your project. The transformation is now under way! The first order of business is to take care of demolition and tackle major structural and mechanical work. Build stairs, move mechanical elements, reroute utility lines, rough in ductwork and underfloor drains, and replace old plumbing fixtures.

Frame your rooms

Now you're ready to frame rooms and install windows and exterior and interior doors. This phase completes the skeleton of your finished basement. The length of time this and any of the following steps requires varies with the scope and complexity of the project, the time you have available to work, and whether you're working alone or with a helper. If you hire out the work, the process moves more quickly.

Room Size Recommendations

When planning your basement, keep these dimensions from the U.S. Department of Housing and Urban Development in mind. The minimum net floor area is within enclosed walls (excluding built-in features, such as cabinets and closets).

ROOM	MINIMUM AREA	MINIMUM SIZE	PREFERRED
Master bedroom	n/a	n/a	12×16
Bedroom	80 sq. ft.	8×10	11×14
Family room	110 sq. ft.	10.5×10.5	12×16
Living room	176 sq. ft.	11×16	12×18
Great-room	n/a	n/a	14×20
Bathroom	35 sq. ft.	5×7	5×9

Install internal systems

After the walls are framed, run wires, pipes, and ducts for water, gas, electric, and climate control. Install nail plates on framing pieces to prevent nails from being driven through utility lines. Take pictures of the lines in place now in case you forget to mark them on the covering drywall. Finally, insulate the walls—including the ceilings and interior walls you want to soundproof.

Add finishing touches

Your project is in the homestretch. Install wall and ceiling surfaces—often drywall, but occasionally paneling or a

Plan for architectural elements before you begin construction. This space includes a wall of built-in shelves, a faux window, and a direct-vent gas fireplace.

suspended ceiling. Then it's time to paint and install trim and flooring. Your basement living spaces are complete. You may have furnishing and decorating to tackle, but now is the perfect time to commemorate your hard work. Have someone take your photograph in the new space. Tuck photos of the project's progression into an album, or use your planning binder as a portfolio to share your efforts and hard work with friends and family.

If space is tight, combine laundry and workout equipment in one room to get the most out of your basement spaces.

Remodeling Checklist

Use this list to determine your current needs for additional living spaces and the items they'll contain, how you'd like to use your new basement rooms, and what amenities and fixtures you have or need. Then prioritize the items you checked using the following number system: 1 = must have, 2 = want to have, 3 = would be nice to have but can do without.

AMENITIES	ITEM NEEDED	ALREADY HAVE ITEM	PRIORITY (1, 2, 3)
Family and Media Rooms			
Fireplace	☐	☐	_____
Television	☐	☐	_____
Sound System	☐	☐	_____
Projector & Screen	☐	☐	_____
Bookshelves	☐	☐	_____
Other Storage	☐	☐	_____
Furnishings	☐	☐	_____
Entertaining Areas	☐	☐	_____
Mini Kitchen or Wet Bar	☐	☐	_____
Full-Size Sink	☐	☐	_____
Bar Sink	☐	☐	_____
Undercounter Refrigerator	☐	☐	_____
Microwave Oven	☐	☐	_____
Warming Drawer	☐	☐	_____
Dishwasher	☐	☐	_____
Wine Cooler	☐	☐	_____
Lower Cabinetry	☐	☐	_____
Upper Cabinetry	☐	☐	_____
Other Storage	☐	☐	_____
Bar & Stools	☐	☐	_____
Game Area	☐	☐	_____
Game Tables (pool, table tennis, or other)	☐	☐	_____
Dartboard	☐	☐	_____
Other	☐	☐	_____
Storage	☐	☐	_____
Furnishings	☐	☐	_____

AMENITIES	ITEM NEEDED	ALREADY HAVE ITEM	PRIORITY (1, 2, 3)
Kitchen			
Full-Size Sink	☐	☐	___
Bar Sink	☐	☐	___
Garbage Disposal	☐	☐	___
Full-Size Refrigerator	☐	☐	___
Undercounter Refrigerator	☐	☐	___
Microwave Oven	☐	☐	___
Dishwasher	☐	☐	___
Cooktop	☐	☐	___
Range	☐	☐	___
Ventilation System	☐	☐	___
Oven	☐	☐	___
Warming Drawer	☐	☐	___
Wine Cooler	☐	☐	___
Lower Cabinetry	☐	☐	___
Upper Cabinetry	☐	☐	___
Other Storage	☐	☐	___
Bar & Stools	☐	☐	___
Dining Table & Chairs	☐	☐	___
Guest Suite			
Bedroom	☐	☐	___
Bed	☐	☐	___
Desk	☐	☐	___
Other Furnishings	☐	☐	___
Television	☐	☐	___
Closet	☐	☐	___
Other Storage	☐	☐	___
Bathroom	☐	☐	___
Toilet	☐	☐	___
Sink	☐	☐	___
Shower	☐	☐	___
Tub	☐	☐	___
Tub/Shower Combination	☐	☐	___
Steam Room	☐	☐	___
Sauna	☐	☐	___
Storage	☐	☐	___
Other Rooms			
Fitness Room	☐	☐	___
Laundry Room	☐	☐	___
Storage Room	☐	☐	___
Playroom	☐	☐	___
Wine Cellar	☐	☐	___
Specialty Creative Suite (woodworking, crafts, etc.)	☐	☐	___

DETERMINE NEEDS

Establishing clear goals for your basement project is the key to successful design. Set primary goals by determining how each person in your family will use the space. The more precise the goals, the more likely the final design will meet your expectations. To help you determine what you want and need, answer the following questions.

- How much time would you and your family like to spend in your basement?
- What will you do when you're there? Would you like to read, watch television, work on crafts projects, run on the treadmill, or operate your business? Would you like it to serve multiple functions?

- Who's in the basement with you? Children, friends, family, or clients?
- What elements will make your basement most comfortable to you? To others?
- How would you like your basement to make you feel when you're in it? Relaxed? Energized? Entertained?
- Will part of your basement serve as storage space? If so, what items will you store?
- When you're in the basement, do you want everything you might need within easy reach? Or are you OK with running upstairs for a drink, a snack, or other items?
- Do you prefer intimate rooms with specific functions or would you like an open, easily accessible floor plan?
- How much money are you willing to spend for remodeling?

Making a wish list

Creating your dream basement is in the details. Give yourself permission to create a wish list. With careful planning—particularly when you work with a design professional—you may be surprised at how many of your dreams can become reality while you remain true to your budget.

As you consider how you would like to use your basement now, think about how you might want it to function in the future. What is your lifestyle like today? How about 5, 10, or even 20 years in the future? At the moment you may need short-term housing for a young adult child who has moved home for a period of time. But what can you include in your design plan now that will make that same space work a couple of years down the road when your child is no longer living at home? Identifying what you can put in place from the beginning may save you time and money in the long run.

The first step in any basement project is to determine how you want to use the space. A comfortable hide-a-bed allows a small lower-level family room to double as a guest room.

With the right design plan an open basement room can serve multiple functions. This new room triples the original size of the old recreation area to make way for a bar, pool table, and spacious conversation area.

This kid-friendly game room includes comfortable furnishings and a miniature pool table that can be moved out of the way when not in use. Flexible floor plans such as this one allow the same space to serve multiple functions depending on needs.

FLOOR PLANS

Make the best use of your basement space by sketching a basic floor plan. Start by doing a scale drawing of the existing basement layout using a photocopy of the grid paper on page 205. One square equals 1 square foot of floor space. Draw the footprint, or perimeter outline, of the basement as seen from above. As you move through this book, you'll revisit, add to, and refine this floor plan. Include existing features such as stairs, windows, and heating and cooling equipment. Note problems such as a planned bedroom with an existing window that doesn't meet egress code requirements. Use the symbols on page 200 to indicate these features.

Obstructions

Occasionally posts, ducts, pipes, and other obstacles complicate basement plans. Carefully map the location of obstructions on the plan view using dotted lines. Moving a partition wall a couple of feet, for example, may allow you to incorporate a structural post within the wall, camouflaging the pole. Locating a half bath next to a furnace may allow you to build a single partition wall that encloses the bathroom and creates a closet to hide mechanical equipment. You'll save time and money by working with and around these obstructions instead of moving them.

In addition to a floor plan, make scale views of the basement interior walls from the side to indicate potential problems and illustrate complex storage systems such as shelves, bins, cubbies, drawers, and other features.

Situating a lower-level kitchen along one wall maximizes cost efficiencies for running plumbing while it minimizes the required floor space.

Make Arrangements

Though you'll likely make numerous changes to the floor plan as you work your way through this book, you're probably already thinking about ways to position furniture in the space. Here are some suggestions for arranging rooms and furnishings.

Direct traffic. If traffic passes through a room, it doesn't have to run through the center. Think of your furnishings as walls or guideposts that can funnel traffic.

Float furnishings. Pull pieces away from walls into close-knit groupings with major seating no more than 8 feet apart.

Keep convenience within reach. Include a handy resting place, such as end tables or short cabinets, for drinks or books near every seat.

Maximize a small room. Use a large-scale piece, such as an armoire or a substantial sofa or loveseat, to anchor the room. Use vertical storage in tight spaces.

Fix low ceilings. "Raise" a low ceiling by drawing the eye upward with floor-to-ceiling window treatments and tall furniture, such as an armoire. Direct traffic away from any low-hanging ceiling obstructions.

Floor plan options

Basements lend themselves to a variety of activities and room configurations. Before you add any further detail to your floor plan, revisit the list of needs and wants you developed at the beginning of this chapter. Next make multiple copies of your basic floor plan. You'll likely want to experiment with a variety of layouts before deciding on the best approach. As you progress, keep all the variations together in a file folder or binder. You may decide an early version of the plan is the best way to proceed. If you keep all of your planning materials together, you'll know where to find them.

Needs first

The best way to begin with the floor plan is by plotting the essentials. If your basement must include a laundry area, for example, add it before you include optional items such as a wine cellar. It's much more difficult to work backward. Starting with the basics allows you to know how much space remains for the extras. Make sure you've marked existing features such as a furnace and water heater.

Walls and dividers

By this point you should have a good idea of what to incorporate in the basement. If not, revisit the first chapter and the following pages in this chapter to define your needs.

A floor plan should begin with a scale drawing of the outline of the space you have available for your basement project. Include all existing features such as stairs, mechanicals, windows, and fireplace. This home is built on a sloped lot. The green-shaded section indicates above-grade areas with natural light; the brown shading indicates below-grade level.

Next, using the plan you've developed, draw in walls and other room dividers that will configure the space. Rather than erasing, use a fresh copy of the basic floor plan to plot out each idea. Allow clearance for swinging doors and adequate-width passageways between areas and rooms.

Exterior modifications

If your plans include exterior alterations, draw exterior views too. Making a scale drawing that incorporates all proposed changes will help show you what your house will look like when the project is finished. This type of project will be complex, so involve a qualified design professional. Having some basic plans to show the professional will help you communicate your ideas.

UNFINISHED BASEMENT

UP

FURN. WATER HEATER

GARAGE ABOVE
20'-0"

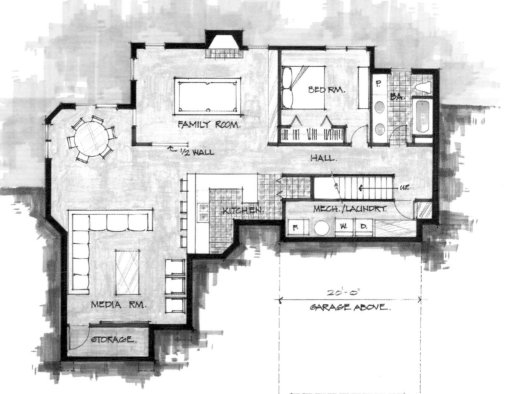

Considering your needs early in the planning process is essential for developing a basement remodeling plan that best serves the interests of your entire family. Note that the footprint for this basement and the one below are the same. Yet this plan is designed for a young family that requires a home office, a children's play space, and an exercise room with nearby shower. Adjustments to the plan, *below*, make the same square footage better suited to entertaining and hosting long-term guests.

Think ahead when designing a layout. This plan provides ample entertaining space now. Positioning the media room in a below-grade portion of the basement will accommodate a front-project system that requires complete darkness. The small bedroom, adjacent bathroom, and full kitchen mean this space can adapt easily as a hospitality suite for grandparents or young adult children later.

FAMILY ROOM.

KIDS PLAY AREA.

DESK. OFFICE.

HALL.

BOOKS.

KITCHEN.

UP.

UNFINISHED.

BA.

CL.

STOR.

F.

EXERCISE RM.

20'-0"
GARAGE ABOVE.

FAMILY ROOM.

BED RM.

BA.

½ WALL

HALL.

KITCHEN.

MECH./LAUNDRY.

UP.

F. W. D.

MEDIA RM.

20'-0"
GARAGE ABOVE.

STORAGE.

BUDGETS

Eventually your basement remodeling blueprints translate into green dollars. A workable budget usually is a compromise between all the great things you imagine for your finished project and what you're willing and able to spend to achieve your goals. Your first priority should be to set limits for the total amount of money you will spend. As a guide, make two lists. One list should include everything you consider essential for your new space. The other list should be the extras—the amenities you'd like to have if there's money left after you pay for essentials. Once you develop your budget, stay committed to it. A commitment to your bottom line will help you make the difficult cost-cutting decisions if your project threatens to go over budget.

Bid basics

As you finalize your ideas and move toward construction, request bids from contractors and other professionals you're considering to complete the work. Convey your goals and budget to the professionals involved in the project. Once you receive bids, add a 5 to 10 percent cushion to the total figure to cover cost overruns and changes to your plans that may occur after construction has begun. For more information on obtaining bids, turn to page 85.

Cost-saving strategies

Your budget should include all of the essentials for your project, but it is possible to save money with these steps.

Simplify the design. Take a look at premium architectural features, such as curved walls or fancy ceiling treatments. Separate frills from essentials.

Substitute less-expensive materials. Today great looks come in a wide range of prices. Some materials—such as certain natural stone tiles, for example—can be expensive. Research flooring alternatives that replicate the look of natural stone; you may find the look you want for substantially less per square foot.

Consider remodeling in phases. Some elements needn't be completed immediately. Prewire for home office equipment and the media room, for example, then add built-ins and electronic equipment later.

Tackle some of the work yourself. Demolition, painting, tiling, and cleanup are popular do-it-yourself jobs. Perhaps you can tackle minor surface regrading as well as handle the cleanup and finish work, such as painting and installing trim.

Sources of Money

Determining how to finance a basement remodeling project is a personal decision. Here are a few of the most common funding options:

Cash. It's the simplest way to pay for your basement transformation. Write a check or use your credit card and pay off the monthly charges.

Savings. Borrow from yourself so there isn't the hassle of paying interest to a lending institution.

Home equity loan. This type of loan borrows against the equity you've built on your home. The rates are fixed, so payment each month over the term of the loan (generally between 5 and 30 years) remains the same. The amount you can borrow depends on your home's appraised or fair market value and the amount you still owe on any outstanding mortgage loans. The interest paid on this type of loan generally is tax deductible.

Home equity line of credit. This form of revolving credit is based on your home's value and the amount of equity you have. With this loan, you have the flexibility of borrowing as you go. Interest rates are variable so monthly payments vary.

Refinancing. Taking a cash-out mortgage loan allows you to refinance your mortgage for a higher overall amount than what you currently owe on your home. The amount depends on your home's accumulated equity and value. Interest rates are lower than with home equity loans, but expect to pay standard closing costs.

Low-cost improvement loans. Available in many cities for developing or historic neighborhoods or for people in low-income situations, these loans are sometimes forgivable. Contact your local building code official, city planner, or historical society to learn more about programs that help cut the cost of financing your remodeling.

The sky's the limit in this basement home theater. A string of tiny white lights behind deep blue acrylic panels creates a starlit sky effect. If your wish list includes special effects like this, consider other places to cut costs to stay within your budget.

PROFESSIONALS

Unless you have considerable design experience, you may wish to enlist a professional such as an architect, interior designer, or a member of a design/build team. A professional will help express your thoughts on paper and offer fresh ideas. In addition the experience and expertise of professionals ensure the project will meet local building codes and may help you avoid expensive mistakes. Although design professionals have specialized areas of expertise, most are well versed in all phases of design and can help create a comprehensive plan.

Architects
Working primarily with the structure and organization of space, architects are familiar with many types of building materials, finishes, and appliances, and have thorough knowledge of structural, electrical, plumbing, heating, ventilation, and air-conditioning systems. Plans that include structural changes to your house and need to be reviewed by your local building and planning commission should be prepared by an architect or structural engineer. Depending on the project and the work involved, architects may charge a percentage of the project's total cost, an hourly rate, or a flat fee agreed upon at the beginning of the project.

Interior designers
When it comes to creating an interior space that meets your functional and aesthetic goals, an interior designer is the person to hire. Traditionally interior designers work with colors, wall finishes, fabrics, floor coverings, furnishings, lighting, and accessories to personalize a space. Interior designers certified by the American Society of Interior Designers (ASID), however, must demonstrate an ongoing knowledge of materials, building codes, government regulations, safety standards, and the latest products. These designers generally are familiar with building codes and structural requirements and can make recommendations for placement of

> ## Locate a Design Professional
>
> To locate a design professional, refer to your local phone book's Yellow Pages or search the websites of the American Institute of Architects (www.aia.org) or the American Society of Interior Designers (www.asid.org).
>
> Although the National Association of Home Builders (NAHB) does not have a national certification program, many states have certification programs for builders and remodelers. In addition, the National Association of the Remodeling Industry (NARI) has a Certified Remodeling Professionals program. To find a NARI-certified remodeler or NARI member, use the search engine at www.nari.org.

partition walls, plumbing hookups, electrical outlets, and architectural details such as built-in storage units, moldings, door styles and sizes, and windows. However, project plans may need approval by the local building and planning commission, and structural changes may require the stamp of a structural engineer or registered architect.

Design/build teams
For complete project management from initial design to completion of construction, enlist the help of a design/build team. Their involvement from the beginning of the project ensures that they are thoroughly familiar with the building methods and techniques specified by the project plan. Design/build teams may not offer the services of a registered architect, so structural modifications will require the approval of an architect or structural engineer. Design/build teams rarely offer interior design services.

The rustic flair evident throughout this lower-level family room is the result of thoughtful planning and conscious design decisions. Involving an architect or an interior designer teamed with a builder should yield such creative results.

HIRING A CONTRACTOR

Hiring a contractor

Unless you have plenty of time to devote to a project and are an accomplished do-it yourselfer, you'll probably want to hire a professional building contractor. Take the time necessary to choose a contractor who has a good reputation and with whom you feel comfortable.

A licensed contractor has completed state requirements to perform various types of work. General contractors usually have a broad knowledge of all aspects of construction and are hired to organize and complete a job according to an agreed-upon schedule. Specialized contractors, such as electrical contractors, are called subcontractors. Electrical contractors, for example, have passed state certification programs that permit them to perform work relating to electrical hookups. It is the responsibility of your general contractor to hire all subcontractors necessary for the completion of your project.

To find a qualified general contractor:

Ask friends, neighbors, or colleagues for the names of reliable contractors they have hired. Get several recommendations.

Meet with prospective contractors to discuss your project. Ask about their experience with basement projects, as well as problems they encountered. Ask for a ballpark figure for the project. It isn't a precise bid and shouldn't be regarded as an agreement, but discussing money at an early stage may give you an idea of how knowledgeable a contractor is and how comfortable he or she is discussing costs.

Ask how long they have been in business and if they carry insurance. Without insurance, you're liable for accidents that occur on your property. Contractors should have a certificate of insurance to cover damage, liability, and workers' compensation. It is acceptable to ask to see the certification before proceeding.

Obtain references from contractors and take the time to inspect their work. Reliable contractors should provide this information readily and will be proud to have their work on display. Check with the local Better Business Bureau to see if any unresolved complaints are on file.

Narrow your choices—select three to five contractors—and ask for final bids. (See "Bids, Estimates, and Contracts," pages 85–87.) Make sure all contractors have similar deadlines for submitting bids—about three

Working with a Contractor

To achieve the best results with a contractor, you'll want a good working relationship. Keep these tips in mind for the smoothest path to finishing your basement.

Frequent check-ins. While it's unrealistic to plan your schedule around when the contractor will be working in your home, try to coordinate a time when contractors arrive every day to discuss the progress. That way, you can quickly assess the work done the previous day and discuss any problems or upcoming decisions. Once you've met for a few minutes, avoid hovering all day—it will slow the work pace.

Open communication. Speak up immediately if you are displeased about anything. The longer you wait, the more expensive and difficult corrections will be. Be clear about what you would rather see, and keep a polite tone. Also remember to express what you're pleased with as the project moves along. Even though you are hiring a contractor to do good work, compliments can go a long way toward getting top-quality results.

Changes in writing. Though you want to minimize changes—they generally are costly—you may need to alter plans after work has started. Write out any "change work" agreements, and make them as precise and detailed as the original contract.

Financial updates. Before the project starts, decide with your contractor how often you'll discuss money. Frequent checkpoints will allow you both to assess whether the project is on budget. No matter how detailed your contract, there may be setbacks neither you nor the contractor can control, such as materials that are shipped later than expected. Be prepared to discuss how this affects the budget and how to adjust the plan to keep costs down.

weeks should be sufficient. Eliminate from contention any contractor who posts a late bid; having too much work is not a valid excuse.

Review each bid carefully to see how thoroughly the bids have been researched. A bid from a general contractor should include an amount specified for the contractor's fee—usually 10 to 15 percent of the total costs.

Take all factors into account, including price, when it comes to the final selection of your general contractor. Be skeptical of any bid that is significantly lower than others—the lowest bidder may not necessarily deliver the most satisfying results.

Make an effort to keep lines of communication open

A general contractor should hire specialized contractors—such as the professionals who installed the lighting, flooring, and fireplace in this basement living room—and should pay them in full prior to receiving your final payment.

once you find your contractor. Schedule regular meetings to discuss progress and keep informed of interim deadlines. Tell your contractor that you don't expect to make your final payment until the job has passed all required building inspections, you have seen written proof that all subcontractors and suppliers have been paid, and you and your contractor have walked through the project and agreed that the job is complete.

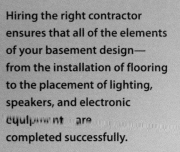

Hiring the right contractor ensures that all of the elements of your basement design—from the installation of flooring to the placement of lighting, speakers, and electronic equipment are completed successfully.

BIDS, ESTIMATES, AND CONTRACTS

Once you have narrowed your list of prospective contractors, you need to get final bids from each. If you hire a general contractor, that person also will need to get bids from subcontractors. In either case, it's your responsibility to ensure you get a carefully prepared bid for the specific project you want completed. Follow these guidelines for obtaining bids, preparing estimates, and making contracts to be sure you find a contractor that fits your budget and will do a stellar job on your basement.

Obtaining bids

The bidding process is the same whether you're gathering a bid on a complete project from a general contractor or on a portion of the work from a subcontractor. Request bids based on your plans from a handful of the contractors you meet initially. If you want to include specific appliances or features in your project, list them and give the list to the bidding contractors. Three weeks is a reasonable amount of time for each of them to get back to you with a bid. When bids return, expect specific, itemized materials lists; a schedule noting what will be done when and when payments will be made based on that progress; and the contractor's fee. Bid prices are not necessarily predictors of the quality of work or materials to be used, so ask contractors to explain their bids in detail.

Preparing estimates

If you'll be doing most of the work, determine costs by breaking work into manageable chunks, starting with costs for waterproofing or insulating; then framing, plumbing, electrical, and construction; then finish work. Rather than shopping at several stores for the best prices on individual items, find one home center and lumber source that offers reasonable prices and top-notch service. Save time and hassle by getting to know the staff at the store you choose. Visit when the store isn't busy, and share your plans with the staff. A good salesperson can become a valuable adviser when you're estimating what each phase of your project will cost.

Making a contract

Once you have made your selection for a contractor, you should sign a written contract. Many contractors have prepared forms. If you are unsure about the specific

Comparing Bids

When it is time to evaluate bids and choose a contractor, make sure to:

Check that each contractor has the same information about your project. Otherwise, expect prices to vary because components won't be consistent with all the bids.

Compare line items from bid to bid. One contractor's estimate for materials may be less than another's because the materials are lower quality. Consider which is more important to you—budget or quality—before selecting.

Be wary of extremely low bids. The bid could be low because it doesn't include all aspects of the job, such as removal of waste from the site.

Base your decision on more than the final cost. Compare the estimated time frame between bids—higher costs are justified if the work is being done on a faster schedule. Be sure to check with references from each contractor and factor that into your final decision as well.

Ask the contractor to clarify or further explain if you don't understand an estimate on the bid. It's better to know and understand all the information before a decision is made.

points of a contract, consult a lawyer before signing it. A good contract should cover these points:

- A precise description of all work to be completed by the contractor and subcontractors and work to be done by you.
- A detailed description of materials to be installed, including specific types and brands of materials and finishes.
- The total cost of the job, including all materials, labor, and fees.
- A schedule of payments that you will make to the contractor. Be wary of contracts asking for large up-front payments—some states even limit the amount of up-front payments made to contractors before work begins. The schedule of payments should coordinate with dates specified for completion of each stage of the project.
- A work schedule with calendar dates specified for completion of each stage of the project. The schedule should include an allowance for delays resulting from delivery problems, weather-related interruptions, and back orders of scarce products.
- A "right of rescission" that allows homeowners to back out of the contract within 72 hours of signing.
- A certificate of insurance that guarantees the contractor has the appropriate insurance.
- A warranty that guarantees that the labor and materials are free from defects for a certain period of time, usually one year.
- An arbitration clause that specifies the precise method you will use to settle any disputes.
- A description of change-order procedures stating what will happen if you decide to alter the plans or specifications after the contract has been signed. The description should include a fee structure for change requests.
- A release of liens to ensure the homeowners won't incur liens or charges against the property as a result of legal actions filed against the contractor or any of the subcontractors hired.

Design Tip

No matter how carefully bids are prepared, savvy homeowners know that a remodeling project usually ends up costing 10 to 15 percent more than estimated. Unexpected problems and changes are common. After hammers start swinging, enthusiastic homeowners often upgrade plans and materials, figuring that "as long as we've gone to this much trouble, let's go further." Spare yourself hassle and headache by anticipating budget overruns.

A basement remodel on the scale of the one shown here may require the expertise of a general contractor and professional subcontractors. You may be able to help by installing stock cabinetry and simple track lighting on the ceiling.

When creating a contract be sure to specify which work you're hiring contractors to do and what you plan to do yourself. If your budget is tight you may wish to paint the walls or tackle the decorating.

DIY CONSIDERATIONS

Hiring a general contractor to complete your entire basement remodeling is the most comprehensive approach to getting your renovation completed—but it's not the only option. You may choose to do some or all of the project yourself depending on your skills, time, physical abilities, and budget. It pays to consider these alternatives to hiring a general contractor before you begin.

Do most of it yourself

If you have the tools, skills, time, inclination, energy, and physical ability, you can save a lot of money by doing much of the work; but before you tear into a big project, do an honest self-assessment. Total the cost of the additional tools, if any, you'll have to buy or rent to get the project done. Account for the time it will take you to order and pick up materials and learn techniques. If you plan to take time off from work to complete the project, compute the cost of lost earnings. Then consider the cost of a potential mistake in both time and money. Miscutting a piece of drywall may cost a few dollars in wasted material and a few minutes of time (if you've purchased an extra sheet or two for such a situation). Miscutting a piece of sheet vinyl flooring or expensive carpet might cost a lot more. Wrestling with heavy materials or trying to work long hours to maintain a schedule sometimes can result in injury, an even greater cost. It actually may be cheaper and less risky to hire out some jobs, such as laying carpet or sheet flooring, or extensive wiring or plumbing modifications. Hiring out allows you to concentrate on jobs that better suit your skills, physical condition, confidence level, and available tools.

Tackle some of it yourself

You may choose to do some of the work and hire out the rest. One way is to act as general contractor; the other is to hire a general contractor. Either way, you pencil yourself in as the responsible party for certain tasks. Be sure to stick to schedule. Here are some strategies for sorting out who does what:

Manage the materials. Order, purchase, and arrange delivery of supplies yourself.

Be a laborer. Do work that requires more labor than materials and skill, such as demolition, excavating, insulating, and painting.

Do the costly work. If you have the skills and tools, and if code allows, tackle the plumbing or electrical tasks, and leave less specialized efforts to others.

Be an apprentice. Ask your contractor to leave minor jobs, such as daily cleanup, for you to do.

DIY Ideas

Even homeowners with generous budgets sometimes like to roll up their sleeves to get the job done. Trouble is, most of us don't have time to do all of the hands-on work, and some tasks require tools and skills that are anything but ordinary. When sweat equity makes sense, by all means dig in, but leave more complicated projects to experienced tradespeople. A do-it-yourselfer might paint, install moldings, lay ceramic tile, install a faucet, wallpaper, and do light demolition. Other tasks many amateurs can handle include:

Simple framing. Home improvement guidebooks can help, so simple jobs such as framing a partition wall lie within reach of many do-it-yourselfers. Complications may include existing electrical or plumbing systems—no one should try these tasks or larger structural framing without training.

Drywall. Hanging and taping drywall is a relatively simple task—if you can measure accurately—though it is time-consuming and a little tedious. The material can be fastened with special cup-head nails. Driving drywall screws with a portable or cordless drill yields better long-term results and allows you to shift or remove and reinstall panels (before taping) without damaging them.

Cabinet installation. Although it takes a serious investment in equipment and training to build cabinets, installing stock cabinetry requires fewer tools and skills. Most manufacturers anticipate the likelihood of DIY remodeling and package installation instructions with the cabinets.

Be your own general contractor

If your skills are more administrative than technical, filling the role of general contractor can be a source of pride. Be aware that this job is also extremely time-consuming and challenging. As a general contractor, you manage the purchase and delivery of materials, hire subcontractors, communicate plans to each, coordinate work schedules and inspections, and pay everyone. Select subcontractors carefully. Most subcontractors favor professional contractors over armchair generals because professionals are more likely to be a steady

If you have the tools, the time, and the skills, you may be able to finish your basement yourself—particularly if the electrical systems and carpeting are already in place.

source of income. Before making the decision to be your own general contractor, talk to other people with skills or time constraints similar to your own and find out what lessons and advice they have to offer. Also check local bookstores and online checklists available for anyone preparing to tackle the task.

CHAPTER 3

Evaluate Your Basement

Solve Major Problems, Learn Building Code Requirements

If your unfinished basement suffers from dim lighting, damp air, and ice-cold floors, make the switch from creepy to cozy by addressing basement ills and investigating code requirements before you make any other steps in the remodeling process. Taking time to address issues now will ensure remodeling success in the long run. In this chapter you'll learn how to spot, identify the cause of, and clear up moisture problems—one of the most common basement ills. There's also information on dealing with asbestos, mold, and radon. Along the way you'll get sound advice on how to repair walls and floors and investigate code requirements. Resolving these issues before you finish below-grade spaces with quality materials protects your investment and yields additional living space that's as inviting, dry, and comfortable as the upper-level rooms in your home.

EVALUATION CHECKLIST

Creating your dream basement starts with assessing the condition of below-grade spaces and correcting potential problems. Begin by inspecting your home's basement and foundation using this checklist. If you answer no to any of the following questions (or aren't sure how you should answer some of the questions), use the information on the following pages to determine what you need to do to identify and solve common basement problems.

Creating a dream basement space, such as this lower-level bedroom, starts with the identification and repair of potential moisture and safety issues.

Basement Evaluation

	YES	NO	N/A
Exterior Elements			
Are the gutters clean?	☐	☐	☐
Do the downspouts extend at least 5 feet from foundation walls?	☐	☐	☐
Is the soil near the foundation properly graded (sloping down 6 vertical inches for a distance of 3 horizontal feet)?	☐	☐	☐
Drainage Systems			
Do you have a sump pump installed (if your house is constructed on a high water table)?	☐	☐	☐
Do you have an interior drainage (or dewatering) system to channel water away from your basement?	☐	☐	☐
Walls			
Are your walls structurally sound?	☐	☐	☐
Are your walls free from damage (including damp spots, cracks, and holes)?	☐	☐	☐
Are all bare concrete walls covered in a cement-based sealer?	☐	☐	☐
Floors			
Are your floors structurally sound?	☐	☐	☐
Are your floors even?	☐	☐	☐
Are your floors free from damage (including damp spots, alkaline deposits, cracks, and holes)?	☐	☐	☐
Windows			
Are the outside bottom edges of all basement windows at least 6 inches above the soil to prevent leakage?	☐	☐	☐
Do your rooms have window square footage that measures 8 percent of the room's total square footage?	☐	☐	☐
Are at least half of your windows operable?	☐	☐	☐
Do you have at least one egress window in each basement living space?	☐	☐	☐
Are your windows damage-free, airtight, and energy-efficient?	☐	☐	☐
Utilities			
Are all utilities, including the fuse or breaker box, easily accessible?	☐	☐	☐
Are each of the following utilities in good condition and properly maintained?			
Heating	☐	☐	☐
Air-conditioning	☐	☐	☐
Water heater	☐	☐	☐
Water softener	☐	☐	☐
Safety			
Is your basement free of mold, asbestos, and radon?	☐	☐	☐
Does each room have a working fire detector?	☐	☐	☐
Are there working carbon monoxide detectors throughout the basement?	☐	☐	☐

SOLVE MAJOR PROBLEMS

Before you begin selecting flooring, wall colors, and furnishings for your basement room, identify and solve any major problems relating to moisture, water drainage, health hazards, the walls, and the floors. The following pages detail some common basement ills and offer possible solutions for overcoming them.

Eliminate moisture

Water in a basement can be caused by something as simple as clogged downspouts or a more complicated scenario such as a rising water table. Fortunately most cures for wet basements aren't costly. Here's a look at the possible problems and solutions.

Condensation or leaks? When warm air comes in contact with cool basement walls and floors as well as plumbing pipes, condensation can occur. If water problems seem to clear up in summer when windows and doors are closed and the air-conditioner is running, condensation could be the culprit. Water collecting on the floor or dampness on walls or pipes isn't always condensation, however. Instead it could be a sign of leaks or seepage.

To determine the source of the water in the basement, tape squares of aluminum foil to different spots on the basement floor and walls, using duct tape to secure the edges. Leave the foil in place for several days. Droplets collecting on the underside of the foil indicate water seeping from outside; droplets on top of the foil point to condensation.

Excess humidity—which can be elevated by such internal sources as a basement shower, washing machine, or unvented dryer—can lead to damp walls, dripping pipes, and mildewed surfaces. To alleviate this condensation, improve ventilation in the basement by installing ventilating fans or opening windows during mild weather. You also can seal interior walls and install a dehumidifier. (For more information on dehumidifiers, turn to page 96.)

If condensation is forming on pipes, cover them with adhesive-backed insulating tape or foam-sleeve insulation. Both are affordable solutions and are available at home improvement stores.

Grades and gutters. Water-soaked soil pressing in on foundation walls is known as hydrostatic pressure. In some cases, the pressure is severe enough to crack concrete. Although small cracks won't jeopardize the integrity of the foundation, they do provide water with an easy path inside. (To learn how to repair cracks, see page 98.) Because both poured and block concrete

Handling Hazards

Hazards may be lurking in your basement undetected. Check for these common culprits that compromise your comfort and safety before you proceed with your basement remodel.

Mold is caused by water damage and high humidity. **Find it:** Growing within walls. **Fix it:** Apply a 50 percent solution of laundry bleach and water to the affected area; be sure to provide ventilation and wear protective gear. If mold growth is expansive, replace carpet, insulation, and other affected materials. **Remember:** Mold is present in some form in nearly all homes. Have mold analyzed by a professional to determine its type and health consequences.

Asbestos often is present in homes constructed before 1980. **Find it:** In insulation that surrounds furnaces and ductwork, woodburning stoves, steam pipes, or boilers; in resilient flooring materials or adhesive used to bond flooring to cements slabs; in insulation. **Fix it:** If the material has tears, abrasions, or water damage, hire a professional to test it. Asbestos must be professionally sealed, covered, and removed. **Remember:** Asbestos in good condition usually won't release dangerous particles and is best left alone; exposure to damaged asbestos may cause lung cancer or other health problems.

Radon is an odorless, colorless natural gas. **Find it:** By testing with a do-it-yourself kit or by hiring a professional. **Fix it:** If high levels exist, seek advice from a radon abatement technician. Solutions involve sealing cracks and joints, and using fans and ducts to circulate fresh air. **Remember:** Because it has been linked to lung cancer, radon at a high level is a serious health threat.

Not all windows have to be operable, but for proper ventilation—and to keep excess humidity to a minimum—you should be able to open at least half of the windows in your basement.

walls are porous, they can wick water into the basement as well.

To solve either of these problems, route water away from the house so it doesn't collect around the foundation and seep inside. Make sure that the driveway, patios, sidewalks, and exposed earth slope away from the house. The grade should drop 2 inches vertically within one foot from the house. Continue this rate of decline for at least 3 feet to create a slope that drops 6 inches.

Another way to ensure that water doesn't soak in around a foundation is to check that gutters and downspouts are clear of debris and in good condition, with no sagging spots that may allow water to overflow. Downspouts should extend at least 5 feet from foundation walls. Lengthen short downspouts or place concrete splash blocks beneath downspout openings to direct water away from foundation walls.

Water table woes. Occasionally a house is constructed in an area with a high water table—naturally occurring water that flows through soil like an underground river. With changing seasons, water tables fluctuate. When they are low a basement appears dry and problem-free. Under high pressure a rising water table can force water up from below.

A thin, barely noticeable film of water on the basement floor is often the first sign of this problem. Test by laying down plastic sheeting for two days. Check for penetrating moisture that dampens the concrete underneath the plastic sheeting.

The best remedy for a high water table is to install a sump pump. For added protection, you also may want to install an interior drainage system that drains to a sump pump.

Interior drainage systems. There are two types of interior drainage systems, which also are called dewatering systems. One requires a 1-foot-wide channel cut into the perimeter of the basement floor, all the way through the concrete. Perforated plastic drainpipe is fitted into the channel and covered with gravel. New concrete is poured over the gravel to floor level. A slight space is left between the floor and the wall to allow weeping walls to drain directly into the channel. The drainpipe leads to a reservoir equipped with a sump pump. Excess water drains into the reservoir and is drawn outside the house by the sump pump. Because this type of dewatering system is installed below floor level, it sometimes is effective in preventing problems caused by rising water tables.

Dewatering Devices

Part of maintaining the comfort of your basement is making sure it stays dry. A dehumidifier and sump pump are two devices that help.

Dehumidifiers remove moisture from the air that can cause condensation, mold, and mildew. They work best if the source of moisture comes from within the house—from using a bath or shower or washing clothes, for example—and do nothing to prevent water from entering the room. Dehumidifiers are rated by how much they can dehumidify and how many pints of water per hour they can remove from the air. Know the square footage of your basement before you purchase a dehumidifier to ensure the appliance has enough capacity to do the job. Most units are automatic and can be set to run continuously or maintain a preset humidity level. Removable buckets or basins catch water. Most have a knockout at the bottom where you can attach a tube or hose to direct the water to a floor drain; with others you'll have to remember to empty the machine periodically.

Sump pumps are rated according to how many gallons of water per minute they can pump and how high they can lift the water. Battery-powered sump pumps work during brief power outages—a must if short, violent storms often cause your basement to flood. Check the battery charge twice a year. Most sump pumps exhaust water through a plastic pipe buried in a shallow trench in your yard. The pipe then carries the water to a street gutter where it flows into a storm drain or to a distant low spot on your property. Connecting a sump pump to a sewer line is not recommended or allowed by some local codes. It can overload the sewer line, especially in homes with septic systems.

The second type of dewatering system does not need an opening in the basement floor. Instead plastic channels are fixed to the basement walls with waterproof glue where the walls meet the floor, much like baseboard trim. The channels direct excess water to a sump pump location. Though adding plastic channels is less costly than opening the basement floor, it is not as effective at intercepting rising water tables as the below-floor system.

Design Tip

For more information on mold, asbestos, and radon, contact the Environmental Protection Agency, Ariel Rios Building, 1200 Pennsylvania Ave. NW, Washington, DC 20460, or go to www.epa.gov.

Interior Drain Systems

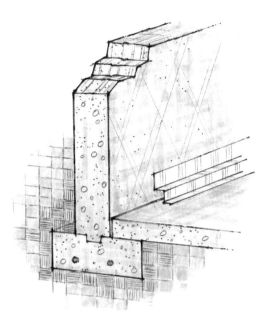

Sump Pump

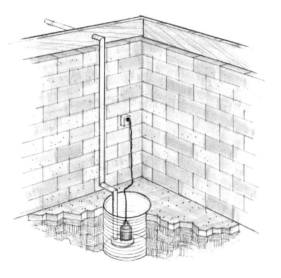

A sump pump draws water out of a sump—a hole beneath the basement floor—so the basement doesn't flood. Combined with tight walls and floors and a dehumidifier, it keeps a basement pleasantly dry.

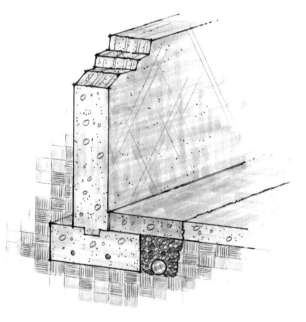

To install an interior-perimeter drainage system, remove the perimeter of the basement slab, dig a trench, fill it with gravel and a drainpipe that leads to a sump pump, then repair the slab (*above*). A less-invasive option is to glue a hollow plastic molding to the wall (*below*), that will trap water and channel it to a sump pump for removal.

A stylish lower-level paint treatment such as this one is only achievable after basic drainage and moisture control issues have been addressed; otherwise, damp walls would have spoiled the effect.

Repair Cracks

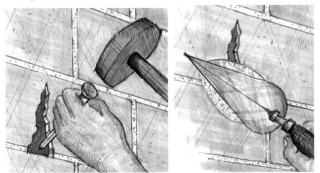

The first step to repairing walls involves chiseling cracks and holes so that they are wider at the bottom than the top (*above, left*). Once the gaps are cleaned, press hydraulic cement into the opening until it fills every crevice (*above, right*). The cement should set even if water is leaking through the hole, but if leakage is heavy or under pressure you may need to hire a professional to install weep pipes that direct the leakage to a sump pump or drain.

Improve the walls

Moistureproofing walls is key in wet basements. To prevent uncomfortable conditions as well as potentially serious damage, repair cracks and seal the walls before finishing your below-grade space.

Cure cracks. The pressure of water-soaked soil often cracks basement walls. If you see a crack line running horizontally across the basement wall, it may be that builders poured part of the wall and allowed it to harden before pouring the rest. In this case have the crack inspected by an engineer. Otherwise reduce the risk of leaks in your basement by repairing cracks in three simple steps.

1. *Chisel.* Use a cold chisel and hammer to widen the bottom of minor cracks and holes. A wider bottom helps prevent the patch from popping out after it sets. The hole should be at least ½-inch deep. Vacuum away any dust or concrete fragments before moving to the next step.

2. *Mix.* In a bucket mix dry hydraulic cement with water until it reaches a puttylike consistency. Work the mixture by hand, rolling it into the shape of a plug when patching a hole or a long, snakelike shape when filling a crack.

3. *Fill.* Press the cement into the opening. Work the material, applying pressure to make certain it fills every crevice. Most cements will set even if water is leaking through the hole at the time of the repair (in which case the water should stop running). Apply pressure to the patch for several minutes to allow it to set.

Seal walls. Once you have addressed any drainage or leakage problems, filled cracks, and thoroughly scrubbed the walls clean, you may wish to waterproof the walls to seal out moisture that could enter through the porous block and concrete surfaces. Consider one of the following products:

- **Waterproofing paints.** When properly applied over a clean surface, waterproofing paints do an adequate job. Oil-based waterproofing paints stop moisture migration yet aren't a completely foolproof waterproofing measure. Latex waterproofing paints have low odor, which is a consideration for basements with limited ventilation, but are less effective.
- **Cement-based waterproofing coatings.** This method, often used to seal swimming pools, adheres well to masonry surfaces. Its thick coating leaves a somewhat rough finish texture but does an exceptional job of stopping moisture.
- **Epoxy-based coatings.** Though expensive, epoxy-based coatings are exceptionally durable. The two-part coatings must be mixed before application; adequate ventilation is essential.

Keep in mind that many sealers work only on bare concrete. If your block or poured wall has been painted, you may have to seal the basement wall on the exterior of the house—a costly proposition because dirt must be excavated away from the foundation to allow sealers and/or membranes to be applied to the walls.

Design Tip

Even sturdy basement walls are under pressure. After a house is built, soil moves and settles around the foundation, placing stress on basement walls. Minor cracks aren't an indicator of a weak foundation—they are signs of strain. If your basement walls are bowing, it's possible to straighten them with steel braces. Consult a licensed home inspector or engineer to find out if your walls require bracing. Then search for "Foundation Contractors" to find a licensed building or remodeling contractor for the job.

Even if you reserve a portion of your basement for storage space and don't finish it like the rest of the lower level, repair wall cracks to reduce the risk of leaks or more serious structural damage. It's also a good idea to apply waterproofing paint to the wall.

A sound floor will allow you to finish your basement with nearly any material you choose. In this living area, rugs soften and warm a chilly tile floor.

Fix the floors

After you solve moisture problems, your main concern becomes the basement floor: Is it sound and level enough to finish with your floor covering of choice? If your floor shows no signs of moisture problems, is level (no high spots more than ⅛-inch in 19 feet), and is not severely cracked, it may need only surface repairs before you install underlayment (in areas you intend to cover with vinyl) or a finished floor.

First check the floor's surface for evenness by rotating a 6-foot level on the floor in sections. Mark dips or high spots with a carpenter's pencil. Repair those areas as follows:

Lows and highs. Fill depressions with patching compound, troweling them smooth and feathering them to the surrounding floor. Rent a concrete grinder to level high spots. Check the surface of repairs with a straightedge, continuing to fill or grind until the floor is flat and level.

Cracks and holes. Fill cracks in the floor using the same techniques and materials used for filling in cracks in the walls. (See page 98.)

Salt deposits. White or yellow alkaline deposits impair adhesive bonding on glued-down floor coverings. To remove deposits, mop the floor with a solution of four parts water and one part muriatic acid, and then rinse the slab with clean water. Muriatic acid is extremely caustic, so follow package directions carefully.

If your floor is extensively damaged and can't be repaired using these techniques—or if such repairs would be too time-consuming—you still have two options. First consult a structural engineer to determine the cause of your floor's damage and confirm that its condition is stable enough that it won't sustain more damage.

One option is to pour and spread self-leveling compound—a liquid mortar—onto a sloped, rough, uneven but structurally sound floor. Most compounds require that you first coat the floor with a primer. Once the primer has cured, mix the compound and spread it onto the floor—up to ½ inch thick—with a floor squeegee. The compound levels itself and dries hard and smooth. For a thickness greater than ½ inch, add aggregate to the mix.

If your floor is not structurally sound, you don't have to break up the old slab and start again. You can pour a new slab right over the old one as long as the increase in floor height leaves you enough headroom (consult your local building codes for minimum ceiling height requirements). First install any new plumbing. Then lay a waterproof membrane—such as 6-mil polyethylene plastic sheeting—over the old slab as a moisture barrier, overlapping edges by at least 4 inches. Then lay ½-inch rigid foam around the perimeter of the floor as an expansion barrier, and suspend 6×6-inch #10 wire mesh on brick or pieces of block to center the wire in the concrete when it is poured. Pour at least 4 inches of concrete and finish with a float.

Design Tip

Concrete slabs are in constant contact with the ground beneath them, so they tend to remain cool. If you plan to spend a lot of time in the basement, choose a floor covering that insulates your feet from the chill.

Carpeting makes basement living areas warm and inviting. Avoid installing carpet directly on concrete, however, because wet concrete is the perfect breeding ground for mold.

LEARN BUILDING CODE REQUIREMENTS

Building codes are specifically designed to protect the structural integrity of your home as well as remove potential threats to your health and safety. Many codes vary from place to place, but the good news is you don't have to become intimate with local codes to plan a basement remodeling. Your local building official is there to help you achieve what you want from the project and obtain a building permit.

For your first visit with the building official, be prepared to describe your project—even if your ideas are rough—and ask what building codes would apply in your situation. Bring along a rough sketch of the available basement space—as well as the location and dimensions of all windows, doors, and mechanical systems—to make your visit even more productive. Don't be discouraged if local codes call for a standard that you don't think you can meet. If safety or practicality isn't compromised, building officials may be willing to make exceptions to accommodate existing homes.

Codes to consider

Many safety elements are governed by codes. For instance, building codes require that a smoke detector be installed in every sleeping room and in hallways leading to them. Carbon monoxide detectors are not always required by code, but it's a good idea to install one near all sleeping areas. Better yet, place one next to the smoke detector in every bedroom. Building codes also govern construction materials for fire safety.

Kitchens and baths and the features that go with them have their own sets of codes, so discuss those with the building official too.

Common Inspections

INSPECTION	WHAT'S REVIEWED
Foundation alteration	Trench, forms
Beneath the floor	Floor, framing, utility lines
Framing	Lumber grade, connectors such as joist hangers
Rough plumbing	Pipe sizes, materials
Rough wiring	Wire sizes, boxes, quality of work
Roofing	Materials, flashing
Energy efficiency	Insulation, window area
Interior walls	Wallboard nailing pattern
Flues/fireplace	Clearances, materials
Gas line	Fittings, pressure test
Finished project	Electrical and plumbing fixtures, railings, furnace, smoke detectors

Here are a few other general features that you'll probably want to bring up with your building official:

Stairs. Tread, riser, and headroom measurements, plus handrail shape and location. (See pages 120-123 for more information on stairs.)

General construction. Lumber specifications, stud and joist spacing, nail and screw types and spacing.

Mechanicals. Electric cable type, number and placement of receptacles, ground fault circuit interrupters, and plumbing pipe material (copper, plastic, steel), size, solder type, venting, traps, and connections.

Design Tip

Once you meet with a local building official, it's time to update your floor plan. You may need to make room for an egress window on an outside wall or move the location of stairs to ensure they meet code guidelines. Make any necessary changes now so you know your basement plan is up to code before moving forward.

It's important to check building codes early in the basement design process so that elements including stairs, ceilings, and metal support posts are sized and placed correctly to meet local requirements.

CHAPTER 4

Create Comfort

Heating & Cooling, Plumbing & Electric, Utilities

After your basement is dry and the floors and walls are repaired and sealed, consider the mechanical elements that make the lower level as comfortable as possible. Some of these items, such as a fireplace, may become a focal point of your lower-level living spaces. Others, such as heating and cooling systems, plumbing, and electrical wiring, are vital for year-round comfort but are best hidden from view when possible. Often the basement is also the location of a lot of the functional elements of the home, such as the water heater and softener. With careful planning you can keep these items easily accessible yet out of sight—so in the end, all you see are the attractive, comfortable elements that draw you to your new basement rooms.

Design Tip

In winter, rooms feel warmer when humidity levels are 35 to 45 percent. During cold, dry months, consider operating a humidifier in the basement to release moisture into the air. Be careful not to let humidity go higher than recommended, however, or you could experience problems with mold.

This lower-level living area showcases a variety of heating and cooling options—vents usher air from the rest of the home's heating and cooling system, a fireplace provides additional warmth and style, and a ceiling fan circulates warm or cool air.

HEATING AND COOLING

Basements are usually cool year-round—comfortably so in summer, a bit chilly in winter. Because basements often are partially insulated by the ground around them, the existing heating system should provide the moderate amount of heat needed to bring them up to comfortable temperatures. It's worth taking the time to analyze the heating and cooling systems now, however, to ensure that temperature-related problems don't crop up after your basement is completed.

You can make your basement more energy efficient by wrapping walls in insulation with R-10 to R-19 values. Basement floors tend to be particularly chilly, so if you plan to use your lower level frequently you may wish to consider options for heating the floors as well. And before you progress too far with your basement design, consider the benefits of adding a fireplace. In addition to providing another heat source for particularly chilly days, fireplaces add striking architectural detail and ambience to basement living spaces.

Heating and cooling

Many basements in homes cooled and heated by forced air already have the ductwork necessary to distribute the warmed or cooled air. If not, a technician can install ductwork relatively easily and inexpensively because furnaces are usually on the lower level. Your basement also may benefit from another supplemental heat source, such as a fireplace. (For more information on fireplaces, see pages 108–109.)

If modifying or expanding the main heating and cooling system in your home is impractical, you still have options. In fact, some of the products listed here and in the chart on page 111 may prove more efficient, especially if you won't use your new space constantly.

Electric heaters of all kinds are usually the easiest and least costly to install but are the most expensive to operate. Electric heat can be an efficient and comfortable solution if you live in a mild climate, heat only sporadically, or heat only a small area.

Baseboard heaters are 4 or 6 feet long and operate on a normal household electrical current. Plug them into a wall outlet or hardwire them to an electrical circuit. Baseboard heaters are quiet and easy to conceal, but they also are more costly and ineffective in larger spaces.

Electric wall heaters feature built-in fans to distribute heat and are small enough to fit in confined spaces, such as bathrooms. Because of the fans, wall heaters distribute heat faster but make some noise. They also

Adding a Fireplace

Before you add a fireplace to your basement plan, ask yourself:

What type of fireplace fits your budget? Although a flickering woodburning masonry fireplace built onsite may be the first thing that comes to mind, it probably is the most expensive option. Consider a gas fireplace—many may be built into a surround as well. Or if you long for the crackle and scent of a traditional fireplace, consider a woodburning steel stove instead.

What do you want from a fireplace? Grab a pen and paper and list the following in order of importance: size, appearance, ease of operation, efficiency, and heat output. This step will help you narrow the range of products you'll want to consider for your building project.

What do local building and environmental codes say? Codes can have a substantial effect on your fireplace plans, so check local restrictions. Some parts of the country with higher concerns about air quality put limits on woodburning fires. In other areas, vent-free fireplaces may face restrictions.

Are there structural limitations or requirements? A masonry fireplace may need additional structural support. Or the spot you have chosen for your fireplace may not be acceptable for conventional venting or running a gas line. Consult with a hearth-product professional early in your planning to avoid discovering that you've selected a fireplace that isn't right for your space.

must be hardwired into your home's circuits. Consider furniture placement when you locate a wall heater to avoid blocking the fan.

Portable heaters come in several varieties: radiant heaters, which produce instant warmth; oil-filled radiators, which produce a quiet, even heat; and ceramic heaters, which are powerful yet compact. These heaters allow you to heat only the area you're using and are an efficient way to keep comfortable if you don't use your new space for long periods of time. The newest ceramic heaters have an electronic temperature control to smoothly vary the output of the heating element and a very quiet fan. Their small size and ability to hold a constant temperature without cycling on and off make these units popular. Be sure to look for a heater that has an oxygen depletion sensor, which will automatically shut off the unit before it creates a hazardous atmosphere.

Direct-vent gas heaters are efficient, quiet units controlled by a thermostat that provide plenty of clean heat. They're designed to heat a room's air and then distribute the heated air with a fan. A pipe exits the rear of the appliance and penetrates an exterior wall to vent exhaust gases and draw combustion air into the appliance.

If you have a walkout basement with large, unshaded south-facing windows, you may need supplemental cooling as well. Consult a heating and cooling contractor to determine whether you need a more powerful cooling system. You also might consider supplementing the current system with a window air-conditioner.

Fireplaces

Fireplaces create an ambience unmatched by any other amenities. When chosen wisely, they provide warmth in cold seasons as well.

Direct-vent gas fireplaces allow you to see the flames and be warmed by their radiant heat. Some also include a fan to distribute warmed air, making them efficient as well as decorative. A major advantage of having a gas fireplace in your home is that if your power fails, it can provide some heat. Regardless of the style you

A tile surround creates a striking focal point for this gas fireplace, which is wired to a thermostat and works with radiant heating to keep the room warm.

This freestanding gas stove requires no unusual ducting or clearance considerations, making it easy to install. A slab of slate functions as a rustic hearth beneath the stove.

choose, you'll find them available in a variety of looks, sizes, heat output levels, and prices. You can choose a fireplace that's freestanding or ready for framing. Plan to connect a direct-vent gas fireplace to existing gas lines; LP-fired models also are available. These units offer a combination of aesthetics, efficiency, safety, and ease of installation. They're vented to the outdoors with a short length of two-in-one pipe that carries combustion byproducts out and draws in fresh air for combustion.

Ventless (or vent-free) gas fireplaces exhaust combustion byproducts directly into the room. They're slightly more efficient than direct-vent units and are even easier to install, but they deplete the room's oxygen supply, produce fumes that can be a health hazard, and are more risky for basement spaces. Some states have banned their use. Most of today's ventless gas fireplaces are required to include an oxygen depletion sensor, a safety feature that warns if oxygen levels in the room are becoming low. For health reasons, you're much better off with a direct-vent appliance.

Wood heat from most **woodburning fireplaces** sucks more hot air out of a room than it produces, so these fireplaces are valued mostly for their ambience. Typically these units feature a firebox of heat-resistant metal, so they don't require the additional floor support that many masonry fireplaces do. They can be surrounded by conventional wood framing and covered with drywall or a veneer of brick, stone, or other suitable material.

Airtight **woodburning stoves** can be a great way to heat your new space, especially if you have a good source of wood to burn.

A woodburning heater or fireplace vents directly through the roof, *left*, or along the outside of the house, *middle*, with a flue pipe that extends above the roofline. A direct-vent, gas-burning heater or fireplace, *right*, vents directly through the exterior wall, making for an easy, inexpensive installation.

These airtight steel, cast iron, or stone units come in a variety of sizes, styles, and colors. Many have a fireplace-like hearth and windowed doors that allow you to see the fire. They're a great backup source of heat and burn quite efficiently, although they do require lighting, stoking, ash cleaning, and the carrying in and out of messy fuel. Unlike built-in fireplaces, you can take woodburning stoves with you when you move, or use them in a different room in your house should your heating needs change.

A warmer floor

If you plan to finish your basement floor with stone or tile, consider installing a radiant heating system first. These heating systems warm the floor and increase the overall temperature of the room, often eliminating the need for additional heaters. Radiant heating systems installed between the subfloor and the finish floor usually have a network of electrical heating cables or tubes to hold hot water. Most systems can be installed across the entire room—perfect for a family room or media area where people like to camp out on the floor—or confined to a specific area, such as in front of a bathroom vanity or bathtub. Like other heating systems, radiant heating is controlled by a thermostat that can be turned on or off, up or down.

Radiant heating systems are available at most home centers. You can install the system or hire a flooring professional to install it.

For rooms where you plan to use other finishing floor materials, such as carpeting, consider installing a wood subfloor with sleepers (floor joists that rest directly on the concrete floor). Use sleepers to protect a floor from condensation or as an alternative to a liquid leveler when you don't want to fix cracks, tilts, or imperfections. You also can install sleepers if you want to insulate the floor. You must install a wood subfloor if your finished floor is the kind that has to be nailed down. (For more on flooring materials, turn to pages 148–157.)

Another option for installing warmer, drier floors is to cover the concrete first with a special air-gap/drainage membrane—an option that can cost 40 to 50 percent less than a wood subfloor. This dimpled plastic membrane acts as a barrier between the concrete and whatever finish flooring you choose, blocking out damp and cold. The dimples provide cushioning and create a continuous air gap over the surface of the concrete, which serves as insulation. The gap also allows concrete to breathe and dry by permitting any airborne moisture to be vented to the wall.

In a basement with adequate ceiling clearance, a ceiling fan helps circulate warm or cool air, keeping temperatures comfortable year-round.

Heating and Cooling Options

APPLIANCE	USE	REQUIREMENTS	FEATURES
Baseboard heater	Heating	• Uses a normal household electric current • Can be plugged into a wall outlet or hardwired to an electrical circuit	• Available in lengths of 4 or 6 feet • Quiet • Efficient • Generally easy to conceal
Electric wall heater	Heating	• Uses a standard household electric current • Must be hardwired to the home's electric circuits	• Built-in fans distribute heat • Installs between studs • Small and inconspicuous • Covered with grill or faceplate that extends about 3/4 inch beyond the wall surface
Gas or direct-vent fireplace	Heating	• Requires a natural gas line • Requires a vent—usually a 3-inch-diameter pipe with an inner chamber for exhaust • Rated by the size of room it can heat; determine the basement's square footage before purchasing	• Some direct-vent types can be thermostatically controlled • Variety of designs • Provides ambience
Electric fireplace	Heating	• Runs on a standard household current	• Available with a variable heat setting to control temperature • Hearth surrounds and mantels available • Some models feature separate heating elements and flames, so the unit can function as a space heater without displaying flames or vice versa • Available with realistic imitation flames that sway and flicker
Ductless heat pump	Heating and cooling	• Requires a hole no larger than 3 inches in diameter for a refrigerant line • Connects two major components—an indoor air handler and an outdoor compressor—by a refrigerant-carrying line up to 160 feet long	• Ideal for conversion projects that require supplemental heating and cooling • Independent source of heating and cooling for rooms isolated on their own thermostat
Portable or window air-conditioner	Cooling	• Should be placed in a window or in a wall opening created for air-conditioners so it won't obstruct daylight or views • Rated by the square footage it can cool effectively	• Distributes cool air best when placed high on wall
Ceiling fan	Circulation	• Requires headroom of no less than 80 inches from the bottom of the lowest portion of ceiling fan to the finished floor; check local codes for specifics	• Variety of shapes, styles, and sizes

DESIGN GALLERY
Fireplaces

Few things enhance a room quite like the warmth and ambience of a fireplace. Whatever the style of the basement living space you're creating, there's a fireplace design to fit your needs.

1. A fan inside direct-vent gas fireplaces helps exhaust combustion byproducts.

2. Cherry paneling provides a warm backdrop for a woodburning fireplace.

3. Stone veneer or rock set in mortar are common choices for fireplace surrounds.

4. Even a simple fireplace looks spectacular with a colorful mosaic tile surround.

5. A black granite surround and silver mantel create contemporary style.

6. This fireplace wall features a wood surround with bookcases, pilasters, and a concealed television.

3

4

5

6

PLUMBING AND ELECTRIC

It's important to make certain you have the proper plumbing and electrical elements in place in your basement, whether you're building a new home or remodeling your current one. This task is much easier if you are in the planning stages of a new home because you can include the proper plumbing lines and wiring where you want them. Even if you are not finishing your basement now, if you are building a new home, and think you may want a lower-level bathroom or kitchen that would require plumbing later, it is much easier to have contractors rough in the necessary plumbing now than to add it after concrete floors are poured and foundation walls are constructed. The same holds true for wiring: If you know you're going to have a media room in your basement later, it pays to do the wiring now even if the room won't be finished for a few years.

As is the case with plumbing and wiring anywhere in your house, be sure to consult local building codes before you begin.

Plumbing

Basement plumbing improvements can be easy depending on how finished your basement is. Hold down costs and save time by locating a basement bath close to existing drains and supply pipes. If this is not possible, the job may require cutting and removing concrete to splice into the existing drain line. You'll want to allow for extra time in your remodeling plan for tearing out the concrete as well as for constructing a wet wall to enclose supply and vent pipes. And be sure to schedule an inspection with a building official before replacing the concrete or covering walls.

One solution to avoid cutting into the concrete is to elevate the new bathroom—if you have available headroom—to create an underfoot space in which to conceal new plumbing lines and a drain. Or if the main drain line is too high for a bathroom in the basement, consider an upflush toilet unit. Once drain and vent connections are made, the units are easy to install and typically use standard toilets. Upflush units also allow you to hook up sink and tub/shower drains. When the bathroom is framed out and flooring and walls are added, the unit is completely hidden.

If you are adding a kitchen to the basement, you will need to install plumbing for that as well. Assuming there will be one sink and one dishwasher, you only need one drain line and one pair of supply pipes. All other connections are made with flexible rubber or copper tubing that does not run through walls.

If your basement floods after heavy rainfall, you may want to install a sump pump while you are undertaking other plumbing installation. (See pages 96–97 for more

Wiring for Technology

Whether you plan to incorporate technology in a home office or media room, or simply want the option of adding electronics in the future, wiring your basement for the following items now will save you from hassles and expense down the road:

Power outlets. Most rooms are not designed to sustain the number of devices people use today, so it's a good idea to install extra outlets. Check your circuit breaker to make sure your home's power lines can take the load. Also, determine where you wish to place your home theater to ensure there is enough power where you need it.

Cable. Consider the cable television's point of grounding when you determine your TV placement. This is often where cable companies prefer to enter your house with the service, and the location where all other cable wires in your home originate. If another portion of your home already is wired, run your basement cable from that point. Include additional cable outlet locations to allow flexibility with the room's future layout.

Surround sound. Include in-wall wires for surround sound before drywall goes up.

Internet. It's a good idea to put at least one Internet connection—either Ethernet or dial-up—in the office, bedroom, and living room. Installing the wiring now avoids unsightly holes in the future and allows you flexibility in the placement of ports.

information.) In addition, if your basement includes a laundry area you'll need to run hot and cold water supply lines to the washer and tap into a drain stack.

Electric

If you are remodeling your basement, the basic wiring already will be in place. Think about how you want to use your basement spaces so that you can run lines to the proper locations for outlets and switches. If you have a larger basement with multiple functional spaces, you'll likely want separate switches to operate lights in each area of the basement independently. Local building codes will dictate at what distance from the floor and at what intervals along the wall outlets must be installed. Think about where you'll want lighting in each room too so you can run electrical wiring to the right spots. For more information on determining where to place lighting, see pages 144–147.

Plumbing and electricity are considerations when it comes to planning a basement bathroom. Lighting fixtures in the shower area must have waterproof lenses.

INCORPORATING BASEMENT UTILITIES

Mechanical equipment—such as furnaces, water heaters, and softeners—often makes its home in the basement long before lower-level living spaces are finished. Fortunately it's relatively easy to hide the inner workings of your home from view.

In older homes furnaces and water heaters often are located in the center of the basement. If possible, develop a floor plan that allows these mechanicals to remain in place. If their location undermines your plans for your new living space, however, it may be necessary, though costly, to move them to a more remote location in the basement. Place utilities in their own room or let

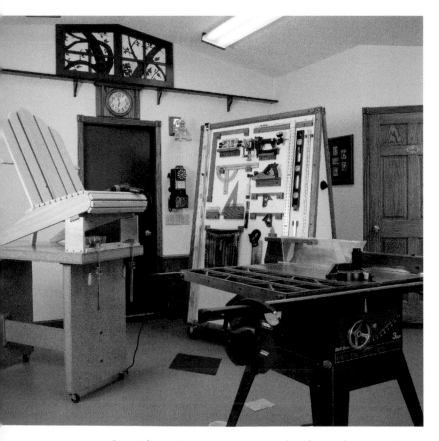

Concealing utilities in a basement shop keeps them out of common living areas. If you create a utility closet, make sure there's plenty of room to access the mechanical elements.

In older homes, the utilities may be located in the center of an unfinished basement. When remodeling, you may opt to move the utilities to a different part of the basement to create comfortable, open living areas.

Energy-Efficient Options

While you're moving your utilities or building them into their own room, it may be a good time to consider upgrading to more energy-efficient versions. Many mechanical items—including air-source heat pumps, boilers, central air-conditioning, dehumidifiers, and furnaces—are now Energy Star qualified. Earning the Energy Star means products meet strict energy-efficiency guidelines set by the U.S. Environmental Protection Agency and the Department of Energy. How does that benefit you?

Saving energy prevents pollution. By choosing products with the Energy Star logo, you help prevent global warming and promote cleaner air.

Energy Star appliances cost less in the long run. Although these products may be more expensive to purchase than others, the cost difference will be paid back over time through lower energy bills.

Your home will be more comfortable. Forget damp, chilly mornings—with Energy Star appliances your home will stay warmer in the winter and cooler in the summer.

To learn more about Energy Star appliances, visit www.energystar.gov.

them share space with the laundry or shop. In addition to common utilities, you may wish to install a whole-house vacuum or humidifier in that location.

Most appliances require air space above and around the housing; refer to the user's manual or contact the manufacturer. Make sure a mechanical equipment room has its own light switch near the entrance. Doors to such spaces must be big enough to move the largest piece of equipment in or out and should never measure less than 20 inches wide. Allow for a clear workspace—30 inches wide by 30 inches tall—near the furnace control panel.

Design Tip

Once you've identified where you want your fireplace, the prime spots for running plumbing and wiring, and the location of your utilities, update your floor plan again. Draw your fireplace, utility closet, bathroom fixtures, and kitchen appliances to scale. You may wish to mark the location of electrical outlets as well to help determine where you'll place the television, lamps, and other electrical items.

CHAPTER 5

Shape the Space

Stairways, Windows, Walls, Doors

With your basement ready for finishing, it's time to focus your ideas and claim the additional living space now within your reach. You've probably spent hours sketching design possibilities on everything from napkins to the back of the grocery list. Now it's time to boil down those thoughts to a few favorites and plan more precisely. In this chapter you'll find guidance on selecting the style and placement of windows, doors, and stairways. Also look at tips on constructing and finishing non-load-bearing and soundproof walls. Once it's easy to access your basement living spaces—and move between new, well-defined rooms— you'll begin to see the potential of your lower-level spaces taking shape.

STAIRWAYS

You already have stairs to your basement, but now is a good time to make sure they meet code. You'll also want to consider how the basement stairs contribute to the space in terms of looks and convenience. If your steps don't measure up to code or if the location in the basement won't allow you to sensibly arrange the room, you can rebuild the stairs or even relocate them. (See "Stair-Positioning Tips," *below.*)

Codes vary with stair configurations and railing shape, so you'll need to talk to the building official about these as well. It's also a good idea to consult with an architect or other design professional to make sure that the stairway style works well with your other ideas. Here are some stair designs to consider:

- Straight-run stairs take up about 40 square feet of floor space at the lower level.
- L- or U-shape stairs require more floor area but are a good choice when a straight run is too steep.
- Spiral stairs are usually only 4 to 6 feet in diameter, so they take up little floor space. If you consider this option, you'll need another route for moving furniture and other large objects into the basement (such as walkout access). Building codes often prohibit spiral stairs leading to rooms larger than 400 square feet.
- Winder staircases eliminate the need for a landing around a sharp turn.

U-shape stairs lead to the basement. The wooden balustrade fits with the home's Craftsman style.

Stair-Positioning Tips

If you're building new stairs or relocating the current ones, consider what living areas the stairs will connect.

Place stairs leading to recreation rooms and family rooms near the kitchen. When you're entertaining, it will be easy to run upstairs for refreshments if your basement doesn't have its own kitchen.

Avoid connecting a noisy area to a quiet one. For example, a stairway from the basement playroom that leads near the upstairs home office may prove disruptive if you're trying to work. If you can't avoid the connection, soundproof the stairwell by insulating the walls that surround it.

Locate stairs where people can reach the main living area without walking through a bedroom or bath.

Build stairs parallel to ceiling joists. This takes less time to install and requires fewer cuts and materials than stairs built perpendicular to ceiling joists.

Slate-covered stairs lead down to a guest suite and up to a master suite. A bright fuchsia wall signals the transition to the private spaces upstairs.

Stair Shapes

The stair design you select may depend on factors including available space, building codes, and the style of your home.

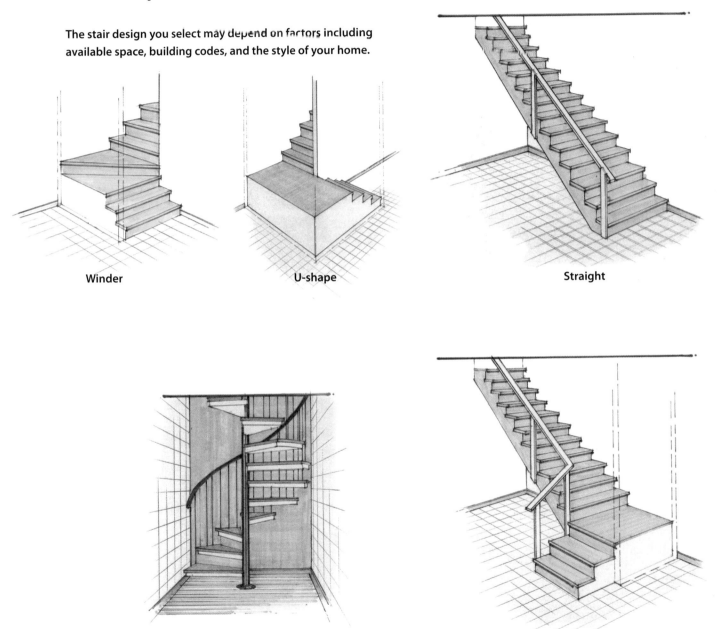

Winder

U-shape

Straight

Spiral

L-shape

A short run of straight stairs may be all that's needed to connect a basement to upstairs living spaces. Here a door can be closed for privacy when someone is using the lower-level suite (not shown) at the bottom of the stairs.

Design Tip

The following are typical building code requirements for a basic straight run of stairs leading to habitable rooms. Always check with your local building codes.

Riser height	4-inch minimum, 8-inch maximum
Riser slope	No greater than 30 degrees
Tread depth	9-inch maximum
Handrail	34 to 38 inches above tread
Balusters	Spaced so a 3-inch sphere can't pass between posts
Headroom	80-inch minimum

White beaded-board wainscoting, woodtone trim and stair treads, and colorful walls lead the way down these winder stairs. The railing features a gridlike design for safety and style.

WINDOWS

Inviting sunshine into your basement will make formerly dreary rooms more welcoming. Your options include replacing small existing windows with larger units or installing additional windows.

If you're including a bedroom in your basement remodeling plans, remember that this room must have an egress opening (see "Window Requirements," *below*). If you want to add an egress opening, examine the area immediately outside the proposed window location for obstructions. Consider privacy, too. If the new window will be close to sidewalks or another house, you can use a fence, wall, or plantings to screen the area.

Welcome light

Adding or enlarging basement windows is not a job for the average do-it-yourselfer. It involves removing portions of the foundation wall and supporting the structure above the wall opening with a header constructed of two or more 2× lengths of lumber. These span the opening and carry the weight of the house. Cutting concrete or concrete block and maintaining structural integrity are tasks best left to an experienced professional.

Most building codes require the outside bottom edge of the new window to be at least 6 inches above the soil to prevent groundwater from leaking in and to keep wood framing members from rotting. The space between the bottom of the header and a point 6 inches above the soil line should be big enough to install a window unit at least 1 foot high. This is a minimum standard, however, and increasing the size of the window will bring in more light.

Window openings that extend below grade must have a window well. Your window well can be 12 inches deep or more and as wide as you want. Installing a window well requires excavating the soil outside foundation walls

In a walkout basement with large south-facing windows, a built-in awning provides shade. If basement windows are visible from the yard or street, they should match the type and style of the home's other windows for consistency.

and installing a retaining wall of galvanized steel or masonry. You may wish to use attractive materials such as limestone blocks or painted cement blocks. Scenic vistas, printed on weather-resistant polystyrene, also are

Window Requirements

Window square footage should measure 8 percent of your room's total square footage. Beyond this general requirement, use these guidelines as a starting point, and check local building codes for specifics:

For ventilation, half the window square footage amount must be operable. For example, a 100-square-foot room measuring 10×10 feet requires 8 square feet of windows with 4 square feet of operable area. If the ventilation requirement can't be met with windows, then doors, louvers, vents, and mechanical devices can be used if your building official agrees on sufficient provisions.

For safe exits in the event of fire, all sleeping rooms above or below grade are required to have an outside door or a window with 5.7 square feet of operable area through which a person can escape. Window wells that are 44 inches below grade level must have a permanent ladder or steps.

Below-Grade Windows

A terraced window well is a great way to
invite sunshine and views into a subterranean
space. Dig the well in a funnel shape, stairstepping
sides and holding back dirt with retaining walls of
treated landscape timbers or masonry landscaping blocks.
Install a drain at the well's bottom to handle water runoff. Plant
the horizontal surfaces with flowers or low-maintenance greenery
for a nice view. To make sure as much light as possible penetrates
the room, angle the exterior framework around the window upward, if
necessary, so it does not obstruct the top of the window. For continuity angle
the sides and bottom of the window framing as well.

available to create a "view." The floor of the well must have a drainage system, preferably a gravel bed and a drainpipe connected to a perimeter drain. If there is no perimeter drain, the gravel bed must be approximately 6 inches deep to hold precipitation until it seeps into the surrounding soil. Install rigid foam insulation between the gravel bed and the foundation to encourage water to migrate away from the wall.

Greenhouse-type windows on top of a basement bump-out are another option and do an especially good job of scooping in natural light.

To capture morning light, place windows facing east. For all-day exposure, point them south. West-facing windows obviously will pull in warmer afternoon sun—something to avoid in warmer climates.

A large double-hung window allows plenty of light and fresh air into a walkout basement space. The white muntins on this window match those on the door next to it.

This walkout basement features a patio door with easy access to the yard and nearby patio. Three awning windows welcome in light and breezes.

Two small windows flanking a fireplace admit some natural light and help make the area a focal point of the room. Other larger windows are necessary for egress.

In a below-grade basement with few places suitable for windows, installing one in the stairway may be an option for increasing light.

Energy Efficiency

Look for the following criteria when buying windows:

U-values. The National Fenestration Rating Council (NFRC) rates the windows of participating manufacturers for the amount of heat that is allowed to flow through a product (its U-value). The lower the U-value, the more energy-efficient the window.

Solar heat gain coefficients (SHGC). A window SHGC measures how well it blocks heat from sunlight, in accordance with NFRC rating procedures. The lower the number, the better.

R-values. Materials with high R-values are better insulators. Most manufacturers apply this measurement to glass, although the NFRC does not offer R-value ratings.

Energy Star. The Energy Star program, a voluntary partnership between the U.S. Department of Energy and participating manufacturers, gives its seal of approval to windows with a U-value of 0.35 or lower and an SHGC rating of 0.40 or lower.

Window Materials

Windows are made of all-wood, wood composites (a mix of shredded wood fiber and plastic resins), vinyl, aluminum, fiberglass, or wood clad with vinyl or aluminum. Each type offers advantages in terms of energy efficiency, maintenance, and cost.

TYPE	FEATURES
Wood	• Energy-efficient • Widely available at home improvement centers • Custom capabilities for making windows or doors in unusual shapes • Requires periodic refinishing • Expensive
Wood composite	• Offers the strength and insulating properties of wood • Less expensive than solid wood • Covered with vinyl or aluminum clad on exterior and paint primer or vinyl clad on interior • Will not accept transparent stains as wood does
Vinyl	• Superior energy efficiency • Available in a few stock colors and some custom colors • Maintenance-free • Can be painted, but then will require periodic maintenance • Moderate cost
Aluminum	• Maintenance-free • Low energy efficiency • Some include a thermal break—a material inserted into the aluminum frames to slow the transfer of heat and improve energy efficiency
Fiberglass	• Combines aluminum's stability and strength with the insulating properties of wood and vinyl • Expensive
Clad	• Combines the energy efficiency of wood frames with maintenance-free coverings of vinyl or aluminum • Moderately priced

Windows are a major expense. To conserve costs, combine less-expensive fixed windows with windows that open, and use stock rather than custom sizes.

Design Tip

Boost your basement's energy efficiency and save on heating and cooling costs by insulating the outside walls. Rigid foam panels are best—foam offers more insulating value than fiberglass in less space. Foam also is ideal when paired with masonry because it's impervious to moisture and water and can be covered with drywall without studs.

This handsome Art Deco-style fireplace wall was created by combining 4×8 plywood sheets of rotary-sawn maple hardwood and solid poplar 1×3 battens—stained dark walnut—to cover the joints between sheets.

WALLS

Foundation walls usually are made of poured concrete or stacked concrete block—not the most attractive surfaces. Fortunately you can cover basement walls quickly and inexpensively. Attach wood furring strips, Z-shape channels, or 2×4 studs to flat, dry masonry walls, then add insulation and cover the strips or studs with drywall. Such treatments give walls a smooth, even surface that accepts finish materials, such as paint, wallpaper, or paneling. This type of wall system makes it easy to install electrical wiring, television cable, speaker wire, and telephone lines.

If basement walls are bowed or out-of-plumb, build a stud wall in front of them to ensure a flat, plumb, finished wall surface. (For more information, see "Design Tip," page 99.) In this case, the stud wall is not attached to the masonry wall. Instead, like a partition wall, the top plate is attached to overhead joists and the bottom plate is nailed to the concrete slab.

To make your basement energy efficient, fill the spaces between the furring strips with rigid insulation. Or fill spaces between 2×4 studs with fiberglass batting. In cold climates, you may want to include a vapor barrier during the insulation process. You should not install a vapor barrier in warmer climates because moisture must move into and out of the house for significant portions of the year.

Partition walls

Because partition walls don't have to support the weight of the house, they are easy to construct and install in virtually any basement location to create separate rooms. This versatility also makes them ideal for camouflaging posts and other obstructions. Standard stud-wall construction is sufficient for partition walls, but don't stifle your creative instincts. Curved walls or walls made

Natural materials such as brick lend visual warmth to basement walls. If a real brick wall is not an option, consider brick veneer, which is installed over plywood attached to a concrete foundation wall.

of glass block are simple ways to enhance a basement.

Insulate partition stud walls that define noisier spaces, such as the laundry room or home theater, or private spaces, such as an office or bedroom, following the guidelines in "Sound-Control Strategies."

Sound-Control Strategies

Building materials are getting lighter, but that makes them more prone to transmitting noise than blocking it. To control sound, try these strategies:

For partition walls, apply a bead of silicone caulk to the front edge of 2×4 studs and top with a sheet of drywall. Secure the drywall to the stud using nails or screws. To this drywall sheet, apply additional beads of caulk that align with each stud. Apply a second sheet of drywall. This sheet, along with the caulk, helps dampen sound.

In lieu of two layers of drywall, install acoustical fiberglass batting within interior walls and ceilings, especially around noise sources such as laundry rooms, bathrooms, and media centers.

Caulk floor, wall, and ceiling edges. Noise can escape through joints where walls meet floors and the ceiling.

Other noise-reduction building products are available, such as acoustical wall framing, floor mats, and acoustical caulk.

Adding textiles to your room also can help absorb sound. Carpeting, fabric on walls, and even upholstered furnishings diminish noise transmission.

This Arts and Crafts-style board and batten wainscoting is made of simple wood paneling. Wainscoting that surpasses 4 feet high, such as this, is appropriate when ceilings rise well above the standard 8 feet. For average ceilings, wainscoting limited to 36 inches works best.

Walls with style

To enhance your basement rooms, look beyond ordinary drywall and consider adding architectural details to your walls. Moldings offer one of the quickest and easiest ways to inject a basic basement with an eye-pleasing dose of architectural interest. Consider adding a chair rail, creating faux wall panels with picture-frame molding, or installing crown molding to define a room.

Moldings come in a variety of materials ranging from pine to hardwood to high-density polyurethane. For simple painted molding designs, paint-grade wood is often the best choice. When ornate detail is involved, however, molded polyurethane may be more economical.

Whatever design you choose, use these tips to make the work go smoothly:

- Choose moldings that complement the existing millwork in your house.
- Mark your designs with painter's tape first; you'll want to examine proportions and check for level. (Mark guides with a pencil before removing the tape.) Whenever possible, choose painter's tape the same width as your molding.
- Get several samples and experiment with layered molding styles.

Creamy yellow bricks from the original basement appear as accents on the new walls and archways in this remodeled space. Yellow-painted partition walls divide the other living spaces.

• Use a miter box and handsaw or a compound mitersaw to practice miter cuts on wood or molding scraps. Measure to the outside corners, and start the cuts from the thin edges toward the thick side. (If you're not confident about your mitering skills, pay a lumberyard employee to make your cuts.)
• Predrill the nail holes to avoid splitting the wood.
• Remember that you can fill and paint over flaws.

When a room lacks architecture, you can create visual interest with a combination of wallpapers, borders, and paints. For more information on decorating your walls with color and texture, see pages 168–173.

Design Tip

Create a special play area for children with a few coats of black or green chalkboard paint on a wall. Section off an area with painter's tape, apply the recommended amount of paint, and remove the tape. For even more fun, create chalkboard wainscoting. Paint the lower half of the wall with chalkboard paint, then top it with chair-rail molding. The rail serves as a tray for chalk, and the chalkboard is just the right height for doodling.

DOORS

A new door with glass panes installed in an exterior basement wall brings in plenty of air and natural light. But creating necessary wall openings is a major project. If you do the project on your own, consult with a structural engineer or building contractor on how to proceed.

First you'll install a header, or lintel, in the opening's top to bear the weight of the house. You'll need to make holes in your basement walls for the doors. If your walls are made of a solid slab of reinforced concrete, this isn't a job for a do-it-yourselfer. Hire a firm that specializes in concrete sawing. You can, however, cut through a block wall with a rented rotary hammer and cold chisels.

If you're fortunate enough to own a house with a walkout basement, you already may enjoy the benefits of good access and light pouring into the space through a patio door. For foundations situated partially or entirely below-grade, you can explore the feasibility of

This below-grade patio ushers more light into the basement and is roomy enough for a chair and collection of plants.

excavating soil to create a walkout. Consult an engineer, an architect, or a qualified builder to find out if your space allows this option.

For quick access from the outside to a basement storage area or workshop, install bulkhead doors, which are set at an angle to the foundation and open to a staircase. The doors lift to open, much like doors used to enter a farmhouse storm shelter or fruit cellar.

In this basement suite, French doors provide a welcome connection to a backyard deck.

Easy Open

When you plan for doors in your basement space, consider these easy design moves that make opening and traveling through doors easier for everyone:

Aim for doorways at least 36 inches wide. This width is much easier for maneuvering a wheelchair compared with the standard width of 32 inches.

Make sure the transition between rooms is bump-free and devoid of thresholds.

A pocket door is a good option for people in wheelchairs. Make sure it has a C-handle for easy grasping and pulling.

Consider lever-style door handles instead of traditional round doorknobs. People with limited hand strength may have difficulty grasping a doorknob, whereas a lever handle can be activated by any part of the body.

In general, install handles at a maximum height of 44 inches to 48 inches.

On the inside

Interior doors are useful for separating distinct living spaces and providing privacy.

Interior doors come in three basic types. Hollow-core doors are inexpensive and lightweight, which makes them relatively easy to install. They come with paintable smooth or molded surfaces made of hardboard. Solid-core doors look and feel like solid wood doors but have a wood fiber core. They offer the style and properties of wood doors without the cost. Plus solid-core doors offer better sound-deadening properties than hollow-core doors and can withstand rougher treatment. Solid wood doors feature natural sound-deadening properties and can be stained or painted. This style of door may be heavy, and precision is required during installation because wood swells and shrinks over time.

Other door style options are available. For instance, pocket doors provide seamless, space-saving division between rooms. Doors with glass inserts keep spaces lighter and brighter, although they don't provide as much privacy.

Door Materials

Doors are made of aluminum, steel, vinyl, fiberglass, wood, or wood clad with vinyl or aluminum. Each type offers advantages in terms of energy efficiency, maintenance, and cost.

TYPE	FEATURES
Aluminum	• Virtually maintenance-free • Cannot be planed, so frames must be perfectly square • Available in a variety of colors • Embossed covers and applied moldings offer characteristics of wood • Many have foam core to slow heat transmission
Steel	• Virtually maintenance-free • Cannot be planed, so frames must be perfectly square • Available in a variety of colors • Embossed covers and applied moldings offer characteristics of wood • Many have foam core to slow heat transmission
Vinyl	• Superior energy efficiency • Available in a variety of colors • Maintenance-free • Accepts paint
Fiberglass	• Superior energy efficiency • Requires periodic refinishing • Accepts stain to mimic wood • Lightweight
Wood	• Energy-efficient • Requires periodic refinishing • Swells and shrinks when humidity changes • Preservative-treated wood provides maximum durability
Wood clad	• Combines energy performance of wood with low maintenance of engineered materials • Exterior clad in metal, vinyls, or polyester • Interior unclad and accepts stain or paint

DESIGN GALLERY
Staircases

Odds are you use a set of stairs to access your basement. Yet even such functional elements can boast serious style that complements your new lower-level rooms, as these striking examples prove.

1

2

1. Carpeted stairs make for comfort underfoot.

2. Storage and seating beneath the stairs maximize space.

3. This sweeping staircase is almost as much about design as it is about function.

4. Open stair treads and railings of braided stainless-steel cable help preserve lower-level views.

5. Spiral stairs provide contemporary style and typically take up less room than other types.

3

4

5

CHAPTER 6

Finish the Space

Ceilings, Lighting, Flooring, Storage

You've identified how you want to use your basement, determined how to address problems, accounted for heating and cooling, and planned the basic shell—stairway, windows, walls, and doors. Now it's time to envision the surface materials—including ceiling and floor treatments—that will help make the space attractive and comfortable. While suspended ceilings used to be the norm for finished basements, here you'll discover a range of ceiling options including hanging drywall, installing wood such as beaded board, or painting the joists. In this chapter you'll also learn how to devise a lighting scheme that will prevent the space from appearing dark and gloomy, and facilitate the activities for which the space is designed. Finally, you'll plan for useful and attractive storage to corral all of the items that likely will accumulate.

CEILINGS

Finishing the basement ceiling may call for a little creative thinking as you figure out how to conceal ductwork, pipes, and other obstructions. You usually can move wires and water supply pipes, but finding acceptable new routes for ductwork or drain lines often is difficult. One option is to disguise or enclose obstructions with a wood framework, then cover the frame with finish materials.

The three primary options for finishing basement ceilings are hanging drywall or wood (such as beaded board or tongue-and-groove siding), installing a suspended ceiling, or simply painting the joists.

Drywall

Drywall creates a smooth, even ceiling and helps give a basement the look of main-floor living areas. However, drywall does inhibit quick access to wiring or plumbing. It is an excellent base for paint and other materials, such as wood panels. For safety, some building codes require that you install drywall under flammable materials, such as wood, because of its fire-retardant quality.

Although you can relocate some pipes and wires so they aren't in the way, you will have to box in large obstructions, such as ducts and drainpipes, with a wood

Exposed joists covered in teak paneling add interest to the coffered ceiling that defines this sitting area and contributes a textural focal point.

This family room ceiling, with rows of bamboo tucked between the beams, draws the eye. The beams were left unpainted to enhance the natural look.

framework. Although obstructions are unavoidable, careful planning will ensure that any boxed-in elements become an integral part of your finished basement.

Suspended ceilings

A low-cost, low-maintenance option is to install a drop or suspended ceiling system. Though these systems have been given a bad name for years, they now come in a number of attractive options, including styles that mimic materials such as decorative tin or wood. This system includes a framework of metal channels hung on wires attached to the joists. (However, some types of ceiling panels are secured directly to the joists.) The channels support lightweight acoustical panels that form a uniform finished surface. The suspended ceiling system has several advantages for basement applications. It's not necessary to move wires, pipes, or ducts, and joists do not have to be straight for the finished ceiling to be flat and level. Accessing heating, cooling, or electrical systems is a simple matter of temporarily removing a panel. You can add lighting by removing an acoustical panel and fitting the opening with a drop-in fixture made specifically for the purpose. Suspended ceilings have the added benefit of insulating unwanted noise from upstairs as well.

Painting

Another low-cost finishing option is to leave all the elements in the ceiling exposed but camouflage the overhead tangle with paint. Painting everything a single color blends the different elements and creates a look that evokes industrial style or fun and funky decor. A paint sprayer will coat everything evenly—including the sides and much of the upper surfaces of various elements. Paint the joists, the underside of the subfloor, wires, pipes, and ducts. Both light and dark colors work well. Dark colors disguise the many elements better while light colors help make the space brighter.

Ceiling Options

TYPE	CHARACTERISTIC
Open ceiling	• Visible beams • Visible sheathing • Visible electrical wiring and cables • Most appropriate for rustic or casual styles
Closed ceiling	• Flat, uniform surface • Concealed electrical wiring and cables • Concealed beams • Concealed sheathing • Finish material follows shape of beams • Maintains open, airy feel
Drop ceiling	• Flat, uniform surface • Concealed electrical wiring and cables • Concealed rafters • Concealed sheathing • Finish material parallel to floor • Creates cozy feel

This cove treatment illustrates one way to add architectural style to a ceiling—a move that makes basement rooms seem more inviting.

The coffered ceiling treatment in this walkout basement game room provides an attractive surface overhead, and thanks to careful planning, the design disguises the typical ductwork and pipes. Recessed can lights illuminate the game table at night.

LIGHTING

Bringing your basement out of the dark begins with an effective lighting plan. Ask the staff at a lighting store or home center to help you plan a lighting scheme that meets your needs. Knowing some lighting basics will help make your visit more productive.

Layers of illumination

Almost any room can benefit from at least two layers of illumination: general and task lighting. You also should consider a third layer: accent lighting.

General, or ambient, lighting creates a uniform overall glow in a space using one central ceiling fixture or a series of fixtures. If you prefer, larger floor lamps and torchères also can provide ambient lighting.

A layer of task lighting backs up the general lighting plan. Target fixtures eliminate shadows and shed light directly onto areas where you work (such as a countertop in the laundry room), where you play (such as a pool table), and where you plan to read.

As you might guess, accent (or mood) lighting occurs when you aim light on an object or surface simply to show it off. For this job you need a lightbulb with a beam that's three to five times brighter than the general lighting.

Lighting styles

Recessed cans offer a means for creating overall illumination, task lighting, and accent lighting. The unobtrusive design allows them to work well in most any room and with any decorating style. Recessed cans are available in downlight, accent, and wall-washing models. Group downlights for general lighting or direct them onto specific areas.

When choosing recessed fixtures for general lighting needs, use open cans without diffusers. You can use a wall-washer recessed can to highlight interesting wall textures, or aim the adjustable lens of an accent light to spotlight artwork (see "Design Tip," page 146).

Track lights are another versatile fixture option. Because fixtures on the track swivel and shift, you can use this form of lighting for a variety of purposes. Now available in stylish models—such as fixtures on stretched wire tracks—track lights offer flexibility to a lighting

This basement living area illustrates good use of a variety of lighting styles. A single overhead fixture provides ambient lighting, table lamps create task illumination for reading, and wall sconces set the scene with mood lighting.

Lighting for Your Home Theater

Use lighting to set the mood in your home theater and as a practical consideration for viewers.

Dimmers allow you to easily adjust the level of lighting. You can turn the lights down when the movie starts yet still make certain there's enough ambient light for viewers to walk in and out of the room.

Install recessed can lights, wall sconces, and lamps to create a soft glow along the walls. These also can highlight artwork or guide the way to the bathroom.

Be creative with bulb options—for instance, try red or blue lighting along the perimeter of the room. The fun colors and placement mimic the experience of a real movie theater.

Small uplights behind or on either side of the screen can make watching movies easier on your eyes. The subtle lighting helps eyes adjust to the always-changing picture.

Pay homage to elaborate old-fashioned theaters with an unexpected ceiling fixture. A chandelier of beveled glass immediately sets an elegant tone.

plan; new track light fixtures can be added as the need for more light fixtures arises. Be careful not to place track light fixtures or any other dropped or suspended light fixture in a location that interrupts the swing of a door.

Another consideration in your lighting plan is how you'll control the fixtures. It's a good idea to put each layer of lighting on a separate switch so you can control fixtures individually and selectively turn on and off general, task, or mood lighting fixtures.

For even more lighting options, place fixtures on dimmer controls, which allow you to easily raise and

Design Tip

When accenting framed artwork, avoid glare on the glass by positioning the ceiling fixture far enough out from the wall so it is tilted at a 30-degree angle and the light beam falls on the center of the artwork. Letting light strike an object from one or two sides enhances the dimensional look, while placing the beam straight in front of the object makes it appear flat.

lower the light level. For example, bright lighting is desirable when you're cleaning or working, but when you're ready to relax, a lower light level sets a softer mood.

Lighting is particularly important in a reading corner. A floor lamp and a recessed downlight with adjustable eyeball trim team to provide task lighting here.

The lighting in this room—including white-painted track lights, a petite floor lamp, and a funky ceiling fixture—provides illumination as well as visual interest.

FLOORING

Unless you install a plywood subfloor (see "Subfloor alternative," page 152), your basement floor is likely a concrete slab. You can apply or install many kinds of flooring materials over concrete for an attractive, durable finish.

Carpet

The softness and warmth of carpeting make it ideal for basement living spaces because it cushions the hard concrete surface below. Installing carpet over concrete is easy; perimeter tack strips specifically manufactured for concrete hold the carpet in place. After you've solved basement dampness problems, you shouldn't have to worry about moisture getting trapped underneath. For an extra measure of protection, seal the concrete with urethane concrete sealer or concrete paint before installing carpet, or try a membrane product. Be sure to choose a rubber pad—foam pads may deteriorate with prolonged exposure to humid conditions.

Ceramic tile

Ceramic tile, available in many styles and colors, is durable, beautiful, and installs easily over concrete. One drawback of ceramic tile in a basement is that it tends to

Vinyl sheet flooring offers an inexpensive option. Modern vinyl wears well, cleans up easily, and comes in a variety of attractive patterns.

These creamy white 4×4 tiles are a smart choice for a small bath. Matching the grout to the tile to blend rather than contrast will make the space look bigger. A sisal rug adds a level of comfort.

This laminate flooring, which requires minimal maintenance, looks like hardwood. Antislip backing applied to rugs placed on laminate floors prevents falls.

stay cool, especially during winter. Consider installing a radiant heat system beneath the flooring to maintain a warmer surface. (See "Warmth underfoot," page 152.)

Vinyl

For a tough, cost-effective floor covering, consider vinyl sheeting or vinyl tiles. These are easily glued to concrete subfloors. Cushion-backed sheet vinyl offers an extra measure of comfort over hard concrete slabs. For any vinyl product, make sure the subfloor is completely smooth and free of defects before installation. Otherwise, imperfections such as cracks eventually will show through the flooring and possibly cause the material to tear.

Laminate

Laminate flooring features a decorative image printed on one or more thin sheets of paper or other fibrous material. The decorative layer, which mimics a variety of materials such as wood, ceramic tile, or stone, is impregnated with plastic or resin and bonded to a rigid core for durability. Today's virtually stain-proof laminate planks or tiles are easy to clean, never fade, and never need waxing. Add pads to furniture feet to avoid scratching the flooring surface.

Wood flooring

People are most familiar with wood flooring as solid, one-piece boards. Most solid wood flooring is not recommended for below-grade installations because it can shrink and expand, resulting in gaps or warping. As an attractive alternative, consider engineered wood, which consists of two or more layers of wood laminated together—similar to plywood but not to be confused with laminate flooring. The top, or wear layer, is hardwood

Design Tip

Regardless of the type of flooring you choose to install in your basement rooms, be sure to keep your basement dry so the floor isn't damaged. Sump pumps and dehumidifiers are two devices that help ensure moisture and leaks don't destroy your flooring. To learn about these options, see "Dewatering Devices" on page 96.

This border isn't as tricky as it appears. It was achieved by cutting a 2-inch square from one corner of each 6-inch tile, and then "lapping" the tiles in one direction. Leave a consistent ¼-inch grout seam between tiles.

For continuity, the same stone tile used on the stairs continues in the sitting area of this room. Although they cannot be used on stairs, rugs are one way to add a level of comfort to living areas if stone is cold underfoot.

These stair treads are dressed in style with homemade stencils protected with floor-and-deck enamel. For safety, avoid high-gloss paints and finishes that may be slippery.

veneer, and the lower layers are usually softwood. It typically is suitable for below-grade installations because it shrinks and expands less than solid wood flooring.

Subfloor alternative

For comfort underfoot or to span an uneven concrete slab, install a wooden subfloor. In a typical installation, ⅝- or ¾-inch exterior-grade plywood sheets are nailed to a grid of sleepers—pressure-treated 2×4s laid flat to help keep the finished height within the 90 inches required by building codes. Correct any unevenness in the concrete by placing shims beneath the sleepers. Fill spaces between the sleepers with rigid foam insulation before nailing the plywood in place. The result is a smooth, even subfloor that will accept most types of flooring.

Warmth underfoot

Two types of radiant floor heating systems—electric and hydronic, or water—are common for home installation. Hydronic systems generally are more popular because they tend to be more cost-effective. These systems pump heated water through a network of tubing. Electric floor heating uses a network of electrical cables to heat the floor. An electric system should be a consideration for a basement because the concrete subfloor will store heat, allowing the system to run less and therefore increasing the efficiency of the system. Most systems can be installed across the entire floor or reserved for a specific area. Like other heating systems, radiant heating is controlled by a thermostat that can be turned on or off, up or down.

In this room padding with an antimicrobial built in can help protect the wall-to-wall carpeting against mildew and mold.

Basement Flooring Options

MATERIAL	PROS	CONS	COST*
Carpet	• Warm • Moderately priced • Readily available • Variety of colors and styles	• Not good in damp and high-moisture areas • Shows dirt in high-traffic areas	$1–$30 per sq. ft.
Ceramic tile	• Durable • Low-maintenance • High moisture resistance	• Cold to the touch • Grout lines can be hard to clean • Unforgiving of dropped objects	$3–$12 per sq. ft.
Concrete	• Extremely durable and long-lasting • Eliminates need for other flooring materials • Can be stained with color	• Cold to the touch • Unforgiving of dropped objects • Plain look of ordinary concrete may require labor of coloring or painting	$4–$10 per sq. ft., installed. Coloring or acid etching is additional.
Cork	• Soft and warm • Natural • Resists mildew • Does not absorb water	• Finish must be sanded off and reapplied every few years	$4–$9 per sq. ft.
Engineered wood	• Shrinks and expands less than wood • Resists moisture and spills • Installs over many substrates	• Can't be refinished • Nailed-down products require subfloor	$6–$11 per sq. ft.
Laminate	• Resembles natural material • Durable • Resists moisture and stains • Installs over many substrates	• Can't be refinished • Sometimes sounds hollow underfoot	$4–$11 per sq. ft.
Linoleum	• Made of natural raw materials • More durable than vinyl • Color extends through entire material	• Requires sealer • Cannot be left wet	$45 or more per square yard installed
Stone	• Natural elegance • Almost indestructible	• Cold to the touch • Must be properly sealed • Susceptible to imperfections	$3–$30 or more per sq. ft.
Vinyl	• Durable • Water-resistant in sheet form • Easy to clean • Less expensive than most flooring choices	• Difficult to repair • Less expensive grades may discolor	$1–$5 per sq. ft.
Wood	• Warm, natural look	• Most types not recommended for below-grade installation • Can shrink and expand, creating gaps or warping	$6–$14 per sq. ft.

*Average estimated cost per square foot. Actual costs will vary.

An area rug defines this lower-level seating area. Underneath use laminate or engineered wood for the visual warmth and beauty of hardwood in a material more suited to a basement application.

DESIGN GALLERY
Flooring

Attractive basements begin with setting the stage and dressing up all the surfaces, including the floor. Discover a variety of materials—from stained concrete to tiles and rugs—to achieve the look you want.

1. Acid stain applied to concrete delivers this mottled marblelike finish.

2. Carpet is a warm, durable, and casual material for this basement family room floor.

3. Checkerboard ceramic tiles set on the diagonal visually expand this room.

4. An area rug defines this seating area. The colors and pattern create a cohesive look with the upholstery.

5. An eyecatching woodburning stove sits atop a fireproof pad required by code for safety.

6. Stone stairs and dark wood floors create old-world style.

3

4

5

6

STORAGE

High on any homeowner's list of desired features is plenty of organized storage, and the basement can yield an abundance of such space inlined storage opportunities. Rather than committing every inch of basement floor space to new living area, make room for built-in storage—perhaps in the form of cabinetry, conventional or walk-in closets, or an entire storage room—as well as portable storage options. Include enough storage space to hold everything you need to store in the room you're creating, plus everything you currently store in the unfinished space.

Built-in options

Built-in storage helps make the most of your basement living space while giving it a custom look. A full wall of shelving and cabinetry, attractively arranged around a media center or fireplace, is one high-capacity solution. Cabinetry is particularly useful for storing items in the laundry room, bathroom, or bar area as well.

Under the stairs

An often-overlooked spot for storage is the area beneath the staircase. This wedge of space can be walled off with a door for access and serve as an ordinary closet. Or think creatively and

Mullioned glass-pane doors make this smart understair hideaway look as if it's always been there. Baskets placed on the shelves become stylish, functional storage.

Floor-to-ceiling cabinetry provides room to store and display a full-scale entertainment center, books, and decorative items while taking up minimal floor space.

This grid of doors hides a large-screen television, audio/video equipment, and a collection of videotapes, CDs, and DVDs. When the doors are closed, the unit forms a stair-stepped wall with space for display.

Design Tip

You can achieve the look of custom-built cabinetry without spending a fortune by augmenting stock cabinetry with features and embellishments. For example, you can remove cabinet doors, paint the interior of the cabinet, and add lighting to create open display shelves or a display niche. Add moldings and divided inserts for unique style and to store specific items, such as DVDs and wine bottles.

transform the space into an entertainment center, built-in bookshelf, display cabinets, or even a desk area.

Out of sight

Another option is to reserve a room for storage only. Wire shelving is easy to install in a variety of configurations that includes special features such as drawers or shoe organizers. Put every inch of vertical space to work by grouping items by size and placing them on shelves and racks of different heights. Choose an adjustable system so you can rearrange easily as your storage needs change.

Design Tip

Many specialty storage stores will design closets for you at no charge. Bring in a sketch of the available space with dimensions and a list of items you want to store. You'll explore design ideas as well as suggestions for specialty features. You can design closets or purchase professional design ideas online.

A hall closet or storage room can stash a variety of items if it's well organized. This modular system fits rods, hooks, bins, boxes, plastic drawers, and more in a tight space.

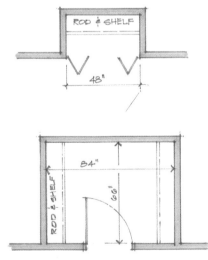

These illustrations show a plan view with minimum dimensions for conventional and walk-in closets.

Maximize closet space with a combination of storage options. This plan features drawers, shelves, and room for hanging items. Custom-built storage allows you to design a system that meets your needs.

The Cedar Solution

Storage shortage is a common dilemma in homes big and small. A basement remodel offers the perfect occasion to boost storage space and include specialized storage areas such as a cedar closet in your home. Discover why a sweet-smelling cedar space saves more than just your clothing's longevity.

Why they work. Orange-red heartwood cedar emits an aroma sweet to humans, yet repulsive to moths and other insects. Without the scent, adult moths invade woolens, quilts, furs, and off-season clothing and lay eggs in the fabric. Hatched larvae then feed on the fabric, leaving pea-size holes.

Installation. Set aside one closet to line with tongue-and-groove cedar strips. Start at the base of the wall with the grooves against the floor, installing right to left or vice versa. Finishing nails and glue or special fasteners hold boards in place. Work one wall at a time, ending with the door, which should be cedar-clad.

Cost. Although cedar materials may seem expensive, consider the investment insurance for your clothing. Expect to pay $1.25 to $1.85 per square foot of cedar plank. For a less-expensive option, consider cedar chip paneling or particleboard. Particleboard is less attractive, but the small amount of glue used in its fabrication doesn't alter its effectiveness.

Easy alternative. Although not as effective, cedar shelves or cedar hanging poles offer a low-cost alternative to a fully lined closet.

A basement may be the perfect spot to construct a large-scale closet or storage room for stowing out-of-season clothes and other items that don't fit in upstairs closets.

DESIGN GALLERY
Storage

Basements are called upon to stash an impressive variety of items, from books and DVDs to children's toys and knickknacks. Make the most of available space with these creative storage ideas.

1. A freestanding armoire on wheels provides portable storage for a variety of items.

2. Douglas fir shelving frames this media center, which has a retractable theater screen.

3. Display cubbies and cabinets follow the lines of a staircase to create a dramatic focal point.

4. This shelving/desk unit provides an entire wall of storage and room for two people to work.

5. A sturdy, portable ladder makes it easy to access items at the top of a floor-to-ceiling bookshelf.

3

4

5

CHAPTER 7

Decorate the Space

Color & Texture, Furnishings & Fabrics,
Window Treatments, Art & Accessories

You're about to embark on one of the most rewarding steps in the finishing process—breathing personal character and style into your new lower-level rooms. Decorating a basement calls for many of the same strategies and materials that work well for upper-level living spaces. Color, for example, makes any room more inviting and livable. On the following pages, take time to look into the art and science of color usage, and learn some of the ways you can spruce up rooms with texture, fabric, and window treatments. Of course, your rooms aren't complete without deftly arranged furnishings and artwork as well. After you bring all these elements together into an eye-appealing package, you can sit back and appreciate all you've accomplished in the comfort of your new basement.

DECORATING BASICS

Decorating is an individual and often eclectic undertaking—above all else, it's about expressing yourself and living with what you love. There aren't any hard-and-fast decorating rules that can be laid out in a few paragraphs. It's about working with your favorite colors, furnishings, collections, pieces of art, or whatever it may be. Regardless of your preferences, the objective is to create comfortable, inviting decor that accommodates your family's lifestyle and the basement spaces you created—whether they are reserved for work, family time, or entertaining.

The walls in this basement living room feature a subtle decorative paint technique that sets the backdrop for a welcoming mix of furnishings, fabrics, and accessories.

Decorating Keys

There may not be any set rules for decorating, but considering some key components will ensure your basement living spaces look as great as you've designed them to function.

Color produces a physical and emotional presence. Whether it's in the form of paint on the walls, fabric on throw pillows, or accents scattered throughout the room, color is often a reasonably priced way to tie together disparate elements, visually stretch a space, raise or lower ceiling heights, alter emotional levels, and more.

Pattern and texture are twin decorating tools that impart style and personality. As you plan, consider where to use pattern and texture, then look to fabric selection, wall finishes, and other items that will help you achieve your look. The more combinations, the livelier your rooms will be.

Fabrics are an easy way to make color, pattern, and texture work for you. If you choose to build a scheme around a dominant pattern found in a rug or on an upholstered chair, for instance, look to other fabric selections that complement that. Or go bold with luxe fabrics on items such as throw pillows—they're much easier and cheaper to swap out later than, say, a couch.

Window treatments can be used to frame your view, block light, and create privacy. Many basements lack large windows, yet you can create instant style by adding treatments to those windows that are there.

Furnishings are key to creating comfortable, well-appointed rooms. Begin by focusing on one or two key pieces, such as a sofa or a pair of love seats. When the major furnishings are in place, it's time to choose and arrange the supporting elements. The most memorable rooms are based on furnishings that relate in proportion, scale, and style but don't necessarily match.

Art and accessories are key design elements for creating interest and personality in a room. For living areas, look for artwork that will anchor the room, as well as smaller accents that work as highlights.

You'll learn more about each of these components on the following pages.

COLOR & TEXTURE

Color can make your basement as bright and beautiful as upper-level rooms, allowing you to make the spaces sizzling, soothing, or charming. Knowing the science behind the hues you love can help you fold color into your decorating plans without fear of creating clashes. Texture feels wonderful to your fingers and feet, and your eyes will love the depth and warmth that textured fabrics and surfaces bring to basement rooms.

Even with most of the walls showcasing neutral hues, a bold accent wall adds an easy dose of energy and visual interest in this walkout basement.

Color lessons

Hold a prism up to the light and you'll cast a rainbow around the room simply by shifting the position of the prism. This mini science experiment is also your first lesson in choosing color for your basement. When white light shines through a prism, it separates the light into the spectrum of colors, each with its own wavelength. Color is the reflection of light on an object created by waves of a certain length, say those of blue, absorbing the rest. The color red has the longest wavelength and violet the shortest.

Color relationships

The progression of color from longest to shortest wavelengths traditionally is presented on a color wheel of 12 hues. Colors opposite each other on the wheel are called "complementary" colors. For a striking and energizing scheme, combine complementary colors—red with green, purple with yellow—because these hues play off each other with the most contrast. If you prefer a decor with less contrast, one using "analogous" colors—those adjacent to each other on the color wheel—may give you the desired effect. "Monochromatic" color schemes incorporate shades and tints of a single hue. A monochromatic blue scheme, for example, might feature navy, royal, and sky blues. Incorporating variations of a

Design Tip

Painting is an easy way to add color and texture to rooms with minimal fuss or expense. You may choose to paint an accent wall a bold hue. Or experiment with decorative painting techniques, such as applying glaze atop a base color with a sponge, burlap, paper, or other material to create visual interest and texture. Painting isn't reserved only for walls—consider painting a checkerboard design on a concrete floor, for instance, or adding decorative detail to a ceiling.

Various hues of brown and lime-green accents combine with striking contemporary results in this lower-level bedroom. White-painted crown molding separates the chocolate-brown walls from the lighter brown ceiling.

Combining red and yellow—two warm colors—makes for a vibrant, sunny basement living area. Choosing a pale yellow rather than a bolder version ensures that the primary colors don't overwhelm the room.

Decorative paint applied to a single focal-point wall adds interest to a small basement room. Here two colors of latex interior paint were double-rolled onto the fireplace wall, while the rest of the walls were painted one of the coordinating hues.

single color can be soothing and sophisticated (cool neutrals) or exciting and vivacious (variations of a hot tropical color).

Warm or cool?

Warm colors—red, orange, yellow—round out one side of the color wheel, while cool colors—blue, green, violet—reside on the other. Blending colors can add visual heat or chill. Green, for instance, can be warmed by adding some yellow—which might take the chill out of a bedroom with a north-facing window well, for example. Or if you're choosing a color for a south-facing recreation room in a walkout basement, you might want to cool down the green paint with a small amount of blue.

Color also has the remarkable ability to make things appear larger or smaller. Warm colors (such as red) seem closer, while cool colors (such as blue) appear farther away. Likewise darker colors advance, and lighter colors recede. Use this knowledge to choose colors for

Calling on the Color Wheel

A color wheel is made of 12 hues: three primary, three secondary, and six tertiary colors. Color relationships built on these groups form the basis of design color theory. Any combination of colors can work together, but understanding the color wheel and some theory makes experimenting with color all the more fun.

Primary. Red, blue, and yellow are the primary hues. These colors are pure—you can't create them from other colors, and all other colors are created from them.

Secondary. Orange, green, and violet are secondary hues. They sidle up next to the primaries on the color wheel because they are formed when equal parts of two primary colors are combined.

Tertiary. Mixing a primary color with the secondary color next to it creates a tertiary color. With each blending—primary with primary, then primary with secondary—the resulting hues become less vivid. Red plus orange, for example, makes an orange-red color; blue plus green makes a green-blue, and so on.

Plywood panels, spiced up with gel stains, lend three-dimensional pizzazz to plain basement walls. When it's time to redecorate, panels like these can be relocated in the room and may be restained or painted.

walls, ceilings, and furnishings, and you can visually stretch or shrink elements to your liking. For example, paint an oversize family room tomato red (a warm color) or forest green (a dark color), and it will seem more cozy and embracing. Add some breathing room to a tiny powder room with walls and a ceiling of sky blue (a cool color) or pale lavender (a light color).

Touchable textures

Texture feels wonderful to your fingers and feet, and your eyes will love the depth and warmth that textured fabrics and surfaces bring to basement rooms.

Texture isn't as dramatic as bold color or lively pattern, but the interplay of contrasting textures—such as weathered wood with fuzzy chenille—adds subtle distinction. Create a casual, eclectic room with rough textures such as Berber carpet, natural-fiber rugs, and twig furniture. Or select smooth textures such as lacquer, glass, mirrors, and polished woods that convey a sleek, formal attitude. The key is to ensure that you don't overwhelm a space with too many rough textures or too many smooth ones. Find a balance by combining opposite textures. Pair textiles with different feels: For example, try feathery velvets with crisp chintz.

Use texture to set the mood in a space. A grouping of fine, soft textures creates a romantic, feminine space; rugged, hard surfaces often are considered more masculine. And textural variety isn't limited to textiles and furnishings—play rough against smooth, shiny against matte on floors and walls too. This may mean placing a shaggy rug over a smooth hardwood floor or hanging a shiny framed mirror from a rough brick or stone wall.

The Language of Color

Knowing a few common terms will make navigating color schemes a lot easier.

Hue is simply another word for color. It's most often used to identify a specific color, such as apple green, grass green, or pine green.

Shade is a color with black added, taking that color from blue to navy, for example.

Tint is created when white is added to a color. Add white to red and you will move from cherry to rose to blush pink—all tints of red.

Tone refers to a color's intensity or degree of lightness or darkness—light green versus dark green, for example.

Chroma is a hue's brightness or dullness. Lemon and butter yellow, for example, have the same tone (degree of lightness or darkness), but lemon yellow has a higher (brighter) chroma.

The subtle interplay of textures in this room—fuzzy rugs on the hardwood floor, a chenille throw draped over a smooth leather chair, even the metallic sheen of the vases displayed in the wall niche—combines to create a warm, inviting basement retreat.

FURNISHINGS & FABRICS

Odds are that you began envisioning how your finished living spaces would look long before you reached this point in the process. But now that it's finally time to decorate, use these pointers on arranging furnishings and selecting fabrics to help ensure that the finished spaces fit your lifestyle and tastes.

Furniture arranging

How you arrange furnishings will influence the comfort level and appearance of your new basement spaces. Think like a decorator and keep these tips in mind as you begin selecting and arranging your furnishings.

Find the focal point. The furniture grouping on page 176 centers on the coffee table, but you can focus an arrangement on any dominant point in a room. When designing a space, first find the focal point. An architectural feature—such as a fireplace, built-in, or a window—is a natural focal point; in rooms without such structural features, create a center of interest with a large armoire, hutch, or bookcase.

Avoid lining furniture along the walls. Even in a small space such as the one on page 177 the furniture can be arranged to promote a more comfortable conversation area. Here the sofa dominates while other seating pieces gather around and make the mix more visually complex. These pieces are only a few feet apart to promote easy, intimate conversation.

Form a natural path. When arranging furniture, it's fine to direct traffic flow, but avoid forming an obvious "hall" through the space. For ease of movement, a traffic pattern can flow in front of the seating as well as outside a grouping. Place chairs no more than 8 feet apart for conversation.

Include tables and lighting. Position a table within reach of every seating piece. Allow enough space to get through by placing the coffee table 14 to 18 inches from the sofa. Choose side tables that are about as tall as the arm of the chair or sofa. If possible, place a lamp near each seating area. Place lighting diagonally across the

A large entertainment center—custom-made to hold a big screen television—tucks beneath an arch to create a focal point in this lower-level family room.

From the rough sisal carpet and sun-bleached seashells to hard metal accents and a soft leather "daybed" coffee table, a touchable—and unexpected—textural mix warms this room.

In this room inspired by world travels, a cushioned bench and intricately carved end tables set the stage, while an Asian water vessel and a Moroccan lantern add scale.

room if you have two lamps. If you have three, create a triangle to ensure aesthetic balance and an evenly lit space.

Fabric selection

Warmth, color, texture, softness, pattern—fabrics can bring all of these pleasing points of interest into a room. Fabrics may be found on furnishings, pillows, floors, and window treatments, but your options aren't limited to these places. When used on the wall, fabric offers a gentle alternative to paper. It also can be used to finish the ceiling in your basement—staple lengths of fabric to joists and hide seams and staples with decorative cording or ribbon, or allow fabric to swag from ceiling beams.

Regardless of where you use fabrics in your basement rooms, remember that they have distinctive personalities. Brocade and damask convey classic elegance, while twill and gingham are considerably more casual. The key in any space is to create a pleasing mix of fabric types and patterns. Florals, stripes, and prints may seem like odd companions, but when combined correctly they can give any room a comfortable, inviting look. The way to mix patterns and prints, however, can seem puzzling at times.

Here are basics that can lead to a successful blend:

Use the principles of pattern. While there are no hard-and-fast rules for mixing patterns, keep in mind that too much of a good thing can overwhelm. When you're

not sure about what works with a particular pattern, rely on stripes to balance your blend. Like solids, stripes mix with everything.

Stay close to a certain style. A bold contemporary print and a small country print, for example, may not be compatible.

Pay attention to scale. Patterns and prints also should complement the scale of the room or the piece of furniture. Petite designs work well on pillows, dust ruffles, and small windows. Large patterns are better suited for walls, bedspreads, and draperies.

Vary scale within a room. Too many large patterns will compete; too many small prints will lack a focal point. If you are unsure, try combining one large-scale print, one medium stripe, one small dark print, and one small light print.

Find the color link. To help you link two or more patterns, watch for common colors. Various motifs will look like parts of a family when they share even a small amount of a similar hue.

Go with the pros. Flip through magazines and books of wallcoverings and patterns to get ideas about what patterns and prints work well together. Many companies offer premixed collections. If you prefer not to go that route, just look for patterns similar to yours and see how the professionals use the mix.

Watch the swatch. Finally you fall for several patterns, but will they work together? Bring home samples or large swatches of the fabrics and wallpapers you're considering mixing. Then lay them out in your room. Or better yet, tape them to the wall. Now live with them for a week or so and see whether they grow on you or quickly wear out their welcome.

Floral-pattern upholstery on the chairs and a variety of patterned fabrics on the pillows add punches of personality to a room with a neutral-tone couch and pale painted walls.

WINDOW TREATMENTS

Even if windows are sparse in your basement spaces, you may want to add window treatments to increase privacy, filter light, and enhance the style of your room. If there are no windows, you can create the appearance of one using lighting and shutters, such as the attractive faux window, *below*.

On the window

There are a number of options for window treatment styles. Valances are decorative curtains used to conceal the mounting hardware at the top of curtain fixtures; cornices are decorative bands that serve the same function. Shades and blinds are fitted treatments used for blocking light and views. Other decorative options for obtaining privacy and light control include draperies and curtains.

Often more than one style is used on the same window. For instance, a window treatment that combines shades, draperies, and a valance might become the focal point of the room. With small basement windows, however, a single window treatment may suffice—try splashing a tiny window with color and pattern using a short fabric valance. Or create the appearance of a larger window by extending treatments beyond the window frame.

This lighting application creates the illusion of a generous window in an inviting lower-level family room; it's actually a frame covered with shutters. Behind the shutters a fluorescent light fixture and a translucent diffusion screen mimic daylight.

In a walkout basement with plenty of windows, wood blinds help connect the space with nature, providing light control without detracting from the view.

Artful selection

The first step in selecting window treatments is to consider function. Keep light out of bedrooms or media rooms using blinds or soft fabric shades with blackout linings. Outside-mount shades provide better light protection than inside-mount versions. Or consider sheers, which allow diffuse light into the room, for basement spaces where privacy isn't as important. Once you've chosen a basic window treatment style, look at fabric and decorative touches.

Design Tip

Eliminate the cords hanging from window treatments by purchasing motorized operating systems, which are now available for Roman shades, roller shades, and draperies. The systems adjust window treatments at the touch of a button on a remote control. Some motorized systems can be programmed to operate at preset times—to open at dawn and close at dusk, for example. The systems also control multiple windows at once.

Two delicate ivory patterns combine in this lush window treatment, which layers a valance over a Roman shade.

Flipping a switch lowers the light-blocking window treatment in this lower-level theater room. A wood valance hides the motorized mechanisms and conceals the blackout shade when it's raised.

ART & ACCESSORIES

After the furnishings are in place, it's time to consider the details. The art and accessories you choose for basement spaces will depend on your taste and the type of room you're decorating. For a recreation room with a pool table and other games, you might consider filling the walls and shelves with sports memorabilia. For an entertaining area with a wine cellar and a bar, perhaps wine-inspired decor and photographs of the Tuscan

Design Tip

To make arrangements of accessories as pleasing as possible, pay attention to repetition, variety, balance, and scale. The principles apply whether you're arranging a collection of vases on a shelf, boxes on a tabletop, or paintings on a wall. You can continually arrange and rearrange accessories to give your rooms new focal points as often as you like.

The art and accessories in this living area include touches of Mexican, Southwestern, and Native American style. Bold colors and heavy, ornate carvings unify the look.

The shuttered wall behind the bed bathes this room in soft light, adds textural interest, and provides a backdrop from which to hang artwork.

Here the Mission-style wainscoting and rail serve as a shelf for showcasing black-and-white photos and souvenirs.

A section of wrought-iron fencing draws the eye to this mantel. Large wooden candlesticks and ceramic vases introduce bolder scale and curvy shapes. They also add touches of color to contrast with the dark leather chair nearby.

countryside look best. Then again, in a relaxed lower-level family room perhaps all you need are framed family photos and well-placed mementos from family vacations.

You may wish to invest in beautiful paintings, antique collectibles, and striking sculptural items for your living areas. But lower-level spaces often are casual, so a few well-placed lamps, some colorful throw pillows, and framed posters may be all you need to enliven basement rooms. Regardless of what you're hanging on the walls, consider the tips for arranging artwork, *right*.

Arranging artwork

Use these simple guidelines to help you arrange artwork like a pro.

Be careful not to hang artwork too high. Decide if you'll most often view the art while standing or sitting. Hang it at the corresponding eye level.

Unite a grouping and make it more impressive by using matching mats and frames; evenly space pictures close together to attract the eye.

Lay out a potential grouping on the floor first. One approach is to arrange pictures so the grouping's perimeter forms a geometric shape. One or two straight lines should run somewhere through the arrangement for the best look.

Make a small picture look more substantial with a wide mat and a large frame. For example, don't be afraid to put a 3½×5-inch print in an oversize mat and an 11×14-inch frame.

Do you like to change artwork often? Prop objects on easels, mantels, tables, shelves, or on the ubiquitous ledge found in the basement of new homes.

Mats and frames don't have to match to make a grouping work. Common colors and subject matter can tie the arrangement together nicely.

DESIGN GALLERY
Art & Accessories

Attractive basements begin with setting the stage and dressing up available surfaces. Discover a variety of accessories—from paintings and pottery to collectibles—to achieve the look you want.

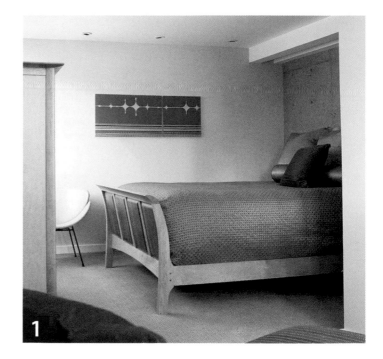

1. A single piece of art, throw pillows, and a funky chair are all that's needed for personality in this guest suite.

2. Here built-in bookshelves offer plenty of display space.

3. A space between the studs was carved out to form a niche for artwork. A spotlight emphasizes the display.

4. Small vases, sculptures, and stacks of books serve as accessories on this shelf unit.

5. Teal walls and bold artwork set the tone in this foyer, which leads to an equally bold basement living area.

CHAPTER 8

Final Considerations

Project Checklist, Family Solutions: One Basement Three Ways, Planning Kit

Now that you have your plan in place, it's time to get your basement project rolling. The start-to-finish overview that follows will serve as a handy reminder as your plans progress. Use the breakdown of the building and remodeling phases to ensure you're on track with your project timeline. Still need some inspiration? Consider the three options for remodeling a basement presented in "One Basement Three Ways"—perhaps one of the plans is exactly what you have in mind. You already may have used the basement planning kit at the end of this chapter to get your design ideas on paper. If not, now is the time to take all those ideas swirling in your head, draw them, and begin the remodeling journey that will take you to the finished basement of your dreams.

PROJECT CHECKLIST

It's difficult to create a general timeline for an entire basement remodeling project because each project will vary in length depending on basement size, available funding, and the amount of work being done. This project timeline is designed only to provide an idea of how much time the initial steps leading to the remodeling work may take, as well as to help you keep track of the steps involved in the actual project.

Design Tip

In the checklist below, the preplanning stage takes an estimated four weeks. For some people, however, this step alone might take a year or more to complete. Many homeowners begin collecting basement design ideas years before they even consider undertaking a remodeling project. Only you can know when the timing is right to move past the initial idea phase of the project.

Step 1 (4 weeks)

PREPLANNING

- ☐ Collect ideas
- ☐ Assess your space
- ☐ Identify major problems
- ☐ Develop a budget
- ☐ Identify financing options
- ☐ Identify possible contractors

Step 2 (4–8 weeks)

SELECTION OF PROFESSIONALS

- ☐ Request bids from contractors
- ☐ Determine financing
- ☐ Select and hire a contractor

Step 3 (4–8 weeks)

DESIGN DEVELOPMENT

- ☐ Learn building code requirements
- ☐ Create a rough plan
- ☐ Discuss and refine plan with an architect or building designer
- ☐ Approve design plan and sign design agreement

Step 4 (2–4 weeks)

PRECONSTRUCTION

- ☐ Select products
- ☐ Obtain permits
- ☐ Prepare calendar of work, material ordering, and inspections
- ☐ Order materials
- ☐ Prepare home for remodeling

Step 5 (4–8 weeks)

CONSTRUCTION

- ☐ Complete demolition if necessary
- ☐ Tackle major structural and mechanical work
- ☐ Frame rooms
- ☐ Install internal systems
- ☐ Install flooring
- ☐ Install wall and ceiling surfaces
- ☐ Do any finishing

Step 6 (2–3 weeks)

FINAL STEPS

- ☐ Inspect the job
- ☐ Ensure everything is up to code
- ☐ Obtain the final inspection certificate
- ☐ Make any final payments for materials or services
- ☐ Decorate—and enjoy your new basement spaces!

The elements that make this basement complete—such as carpeting on the floor and shutters on the windows— probably were installed at the end of the construction phase.

FAMILY SOLUTIONS: ONE BASEMENT, THREE WAYS

Basement projects are as unique as the people who plan them. An individual or couple without children at home has specific needs and wants for additional space that are likely quite different than those of a family with young children. And a family with older children or teens probably has yet another set of requirements for new basement spaces. Even so, all three of these types of families could be working within a similar basement footprint. Here you'll see how the same basement space can be configured and arranged in unique ways to best address the particular needs of three families. As with any area in the house, how a space ultimately functions depends on the size and shape of the rooms as well as the type, size, and arrangement of the amenities and the furnishings.

Family one

Empty nesters with three grown children and grandchildren. Semiretired, one of the homeowners needs an office at home for keeping up with business, on average, 10–20 hours per week. The other enjoys hobbies and wants a dedicated space for projects without the accompanying clutter spreading through the more formal areas on the main level of the house. At least once a month one of the couple's grown children and family come from out of town to visit for the weekend.

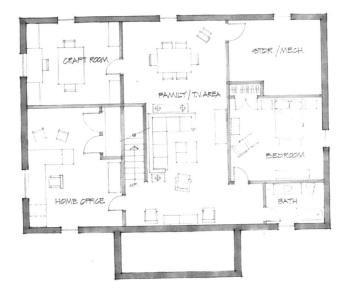

Wall Color

Floor Tile

Craft Room

Wall Color

Carpet

Home Office

The solution

The central section of the basement is designed for TV viewing and relaxing. A queen-size sofa bed is ideal when grandchildren spend the weekend, and a centrally positioned ottoman opens for interior storage of extra blankets and sheets. The chair next to the sofa swivels to allow easy positioning for conversation or for viewing media. A flat-screen TV on the opposite wall is hung above a low storage unit that houses media equipment including a DVD and video games for the grandchildren. Task lighting rests on a small table at one end of the sectional sofa and on the console table behind the sofa. The position of the console table also visually divides the long, narrow room into a conversation area and a space for board games on a table that's perfect for late-night pizza too.

The crafts room at the far left corner of the basement is spacious and features easy-care surfaces and amenities. The floor is covered with eco-friendly linoleum that's easy to clean. A large worktable with shelf underneath is positioned in the center of the room for access all around. Two bookcases on either side of the door house the homeowner's extensive collection of crafts books. On the window wall a desk flanked by two low cabinets with drawers offers ample storage for fabric, thread, scissors, patterns, and other crafting tools and materials.

The home office is thoughtfully located adjacent to the stairs to allow clients to access the office without walking through more private living areas in the basement. An L-shape laminate countertop provides plenty of workspace. File cabinets at each end store hanging files. The built-in closet is outfitted with shelves to house paper and books, and a bookcase offers additional storage. A broadloom carpet gives warm comfort underfoot and provides a low-pile, even surface that will be easy for the homeowners to maneuver as they grow older.

Opposite the office is a guest room with queen-size bed and adjacent full bathroom. Two dressers and a built-in closet for hanging garments mean overnight guests do not live out of suitcases. A small chair and ottoman in the corner create a private spot for reading or relaxing.

FAMILY SOLUTIONS: ONE BASEMENT, THREE WAYS

Family two

Young family with two small children. The family wants a safe, fun place for the kids to play with plenty of room for all the toys and gear that go along with youngsters. With a hectic family schedule, the parents need a large laundry area ideally with a view of the children's play space, so they can do laundry and ironing while supervising playtime. The budget-conscious parents would like the space to work for this young family now but easily transition into an entertainment space for movies, games, and gatherings when the kids are older.

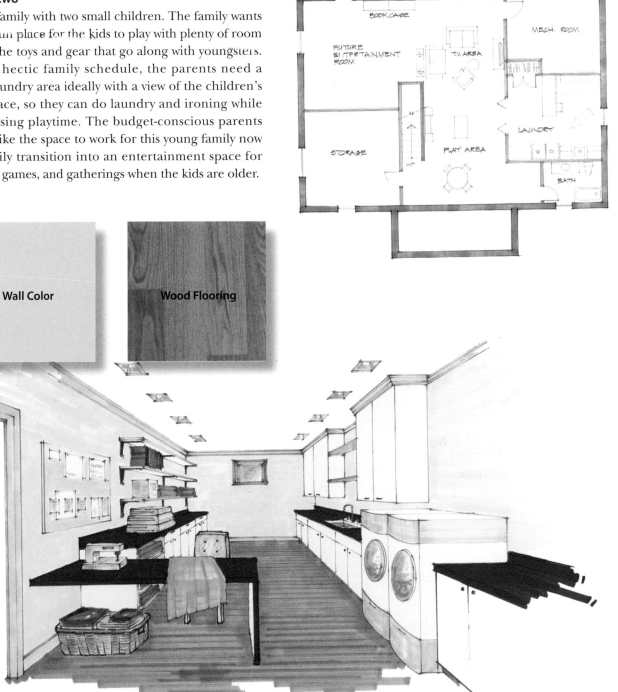

Laundry Room

The solution

This budget-conscious setup provides everything the parents want now and easily can be upgraded to meet the family's needs in the years to come. A large laundry area resides behind bifold doors that close across an extra-wide 6-foot opening to ensure that while mom and dad take care of household chores they also can supervise playtime. The play area features a small table and chairs ideal for little ones' activities. Carpet squares—a practical flooring solution—create a colorful "area rug" in the main play area. Individual squares can be removed and replaced if one of the squares gets dirty, maximizing the longevity of the carpet.

Kid-friendly storage along the stair wall and under the low activity table in the center of the room encourages the children to put toys away when playtime is over. A small media area offers pint-size and adult seating for watching family movies.

Two open areas plus space in the mechanical room provide loads of additional storage—essential for this young family. In the future, the space at the back of the family room will be developed into a media/entertainment area, and the storage room can be converted to a guest bedroom or crafts room. A full bathroom means kids don't have to interrupt play for long and makes for easy cleanup after messy play.

Wall Color

Furniture Fabric

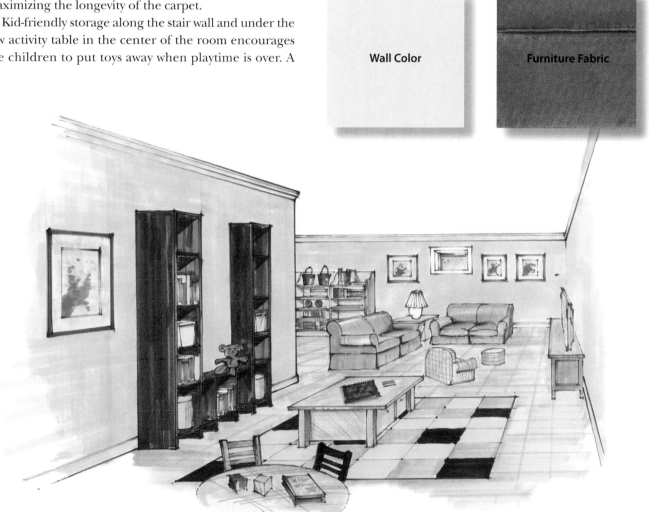

Play Area/Family Room

FAMILY SOLUTIONS: ONE BASEMENT, THREE WAYS

Family three

Family with two children in their early teens. The parents love to entertain and the kids like to have friends over, often for slumber parties. Everyone in the family enjoys movies and video games, so plenty of space for entertaining and media is a must. Though the family enjoys spending time together, it's also important for everyone to have space of his/her own.

The solution

From the moment this family enters the basement living area, it's all about entertainment for all ages. A foosball

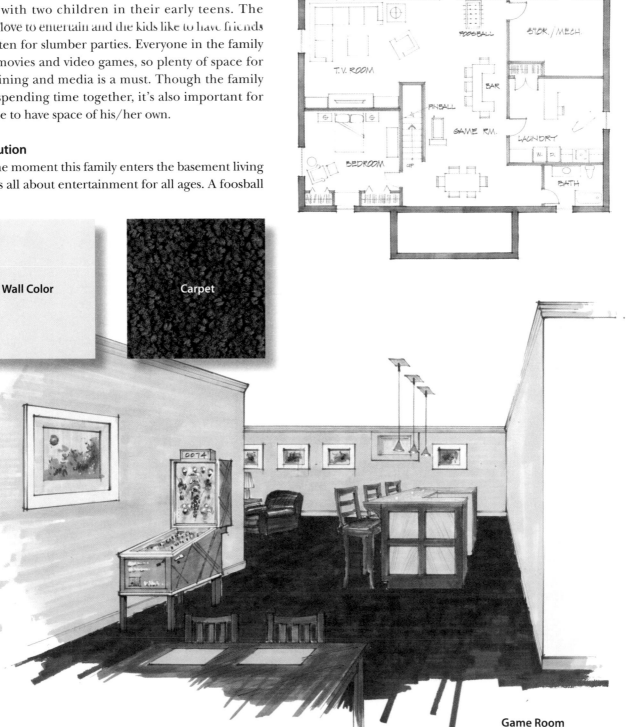

Wall Color

Carpet

Game Room

table and pinball machine, as well as a large table for games, provide opportunities for fun in the main living space. A bar in the same area makes it easy to serve up soft drinks and simple snacks. To the left of the game area, an entertainment zone includes a sectional sofa and pullout bed that are perfect for slumber parties. A leather recliner offers additional comfy seating and easy viewing of the media center with flat-screen TV and media storage positioned along one wall. Extra seating to accommodate large gatherings is available in the form of four stools that tuck under the coffee table when not in use.

An ample, well-appointed laundry room easily handles any mess this active family can generate. An extra-deep counter is designed for folding clothes. A built-in sewing area allows for quick clothing repairs and can double as a spot for doing crafts projects. Plenty of storage options—shelves, hanging rods, and drawers—mean laundry won't end up in a pile on the floor.

A fully appointed guest room provides additional space for sleepovers and slumber parties. This room—large enough to include a wall closet, triple dresser and mirror, two nightstands, and chair and ottoman—in the future can provide semiprivate living space should one of the children come back home for an extended stay while job hunting. A full bath completes this family-friendly basement space.

Wall Color

Furniture Fabric

Media Room

PLANNING KIT

To transform your basement dreams into reality, consider the details. Sketch out some ideas of your own with the planning kit on this and the following pages—it will come in handy even if you work with a designer later.

Plot the space

Use a photocopier to reproduce the planning grid on page 205 at its original size, then copy and cut out the templates on pages 200–204 with a crafts knife or scissors to design your basement. One square on the grid equals one square foot of floor space. The templates include plan-view (top-down) perspectives, allowing you to create floor plans. Plot the entire lower level, including any closets and rooms you'd like to make.

One of the keys to making your basement functional is good placement of doors, windows, walls, and stairways. Use the provided symbols to position existing architectural features. Use a different color to indicate features such as built-ins and furniture that you plan to add. If you have furniture or special features that aren't

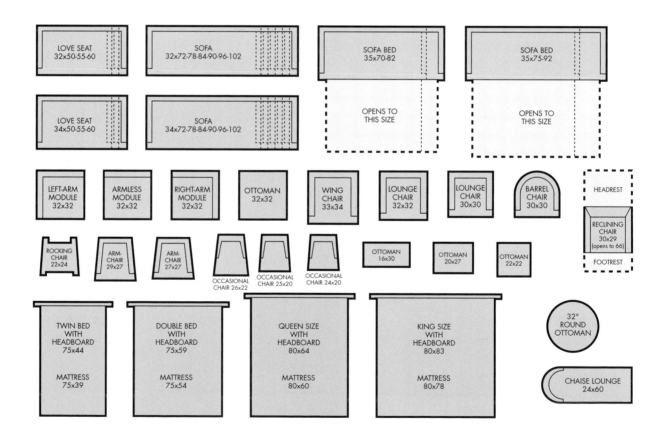

included in the templates, draw them to scale on the grid paper. Mark obstructions, including prominent light fixtures and support posts, with dotted lines. Pay attention to details such as door swings and drawer extensions (marked in dotted lines on these templates) as you consider the placement of these items in your basement spaces.

See pages 74–77 for more information on creating a floor plan.

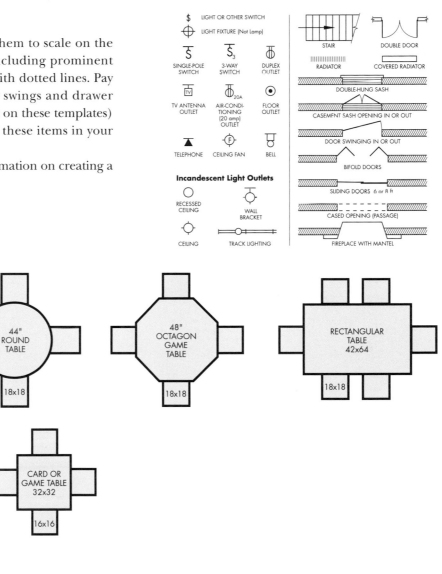

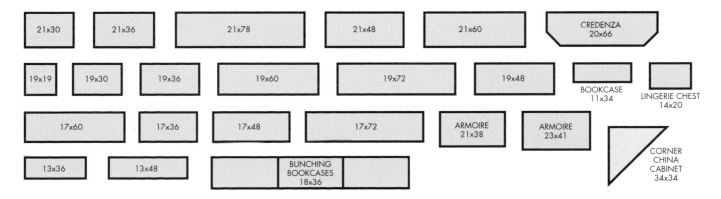

Base Cabinets

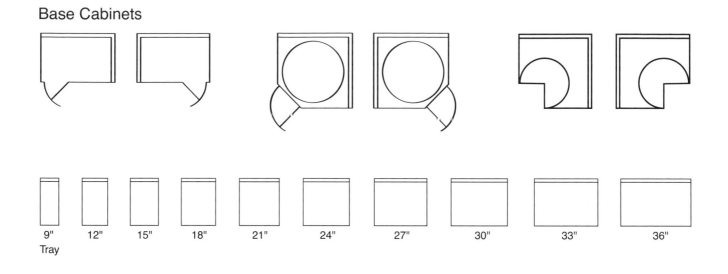

9" Tray	12"	15"	18"	21"	24"	27"	30"	33"	36"

Sink Bases

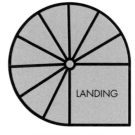

36"	48"	30"

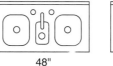

4-FOOT DIAMETER
SPIRAL STAIR

5-FOOT DIAMETER
SPIRAL STAIR

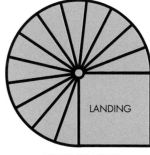

6-FOOT DIAMETER
SPIRAL STAIR

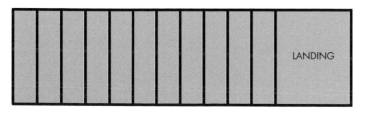

4-FOOT-WIDE STAIR OPENING

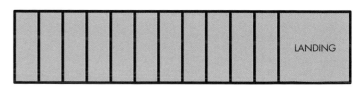

3-FOOT-WIDE STAIR OPENING

Appliances

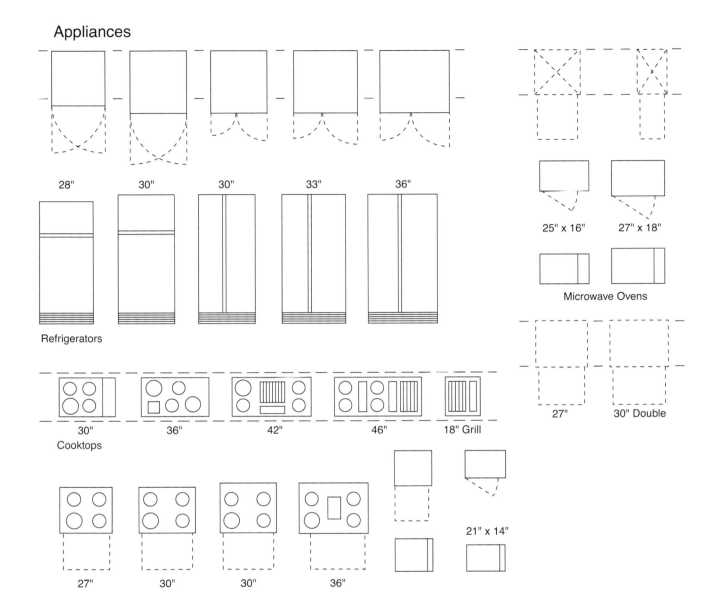

28"   30"   30"   33"   36"

Refrigerators

25" x 16"   27" x 18"

Microwave Ovens

30"   36"   42"   46"   18" Grill

Cooktops

27"   30" Double

27"   30"   30"   36"

21" x 14"

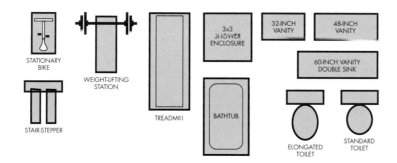

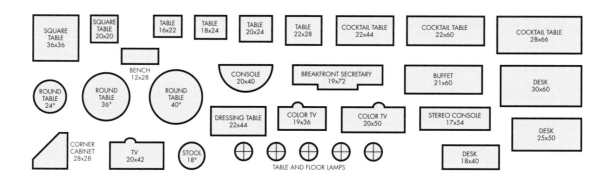

CHAPTER 9

Resources

Resource Guide, Glossary, Index

Planning and finishing basement spaces that meet your needs—and that include a healthy dose of the amenities you desire—requires working through numerous steps and making what can seem to be almost endless decisions at times. Because finishing a basement is a complex undertaking, you'll likely want to involve professionals in some or all phases of the project. Listed on the following pages are names and contact information for some of the many associations and organizations involved in residential remodel projects. Turn to these groups in addition to local resources for assistance. You'll also find professionals and sources listed for some of the basements featured in this book. Addresses and phone numbers have been verified, but the availability of services, products, and materials cannot be guaranteed.

RESOURCE GUIDE

Remodeling Resources

American Homeowners Foundation
6776 Little Falls Rd.
Arlington, VA 22213
703/536-7776
800/489-7776   www.americanhomeowners.org

American Institute of Architects
1735 New York Ave. NW
Washington, DC 20006
202/626-7300
800/242-3837   www.aia.org

American Society of Interior Designers
608 Massachusetts Ave. NE
Washington, DC 20002
202/546-3480   www.asid.org

ENERGY STAR
U.S. Environmental Protection Agency
Climate Protection Partnerships Division
1200 Pennsylvania Ave. NW
Washington, DC 20460
202/343-9190
888/782-7937   www.energystar.gov

National Association of Home Builders Remodelers
Council
1201 15th St. NW
Washington, DC 20005
800/368-5242   www.nahb.org

National Association of the Remodeling Industry
780 Lee St., Suite 200
Des Plaines, IL 60016
800/611-6274   www.nari.org

National Kitchen and Bath Association
687 Willow Grove St.
Hackettstown, NJ 07840
          ⁹-6522   www.nkba.org

U.S. Department of Housing and Urban Development
451 Seventh St. SW
Washington, DC 20410
202/708-1112   www.hud.gov

U.S. Environmental Protection Agency
Ariel Rios Building
1200 Pennsylvania Ave. NW
Washington, DC 20460   www.epa.gov

Contributors and Professionals

Pages 27, 45, 54 (left), 62 (bottom), 137 (left)
Field editor: Elaine St. Louis
Photographer: J. Curtis
Architect: Kathy Eichelberger Jones, ArchStyle, Inc.;
539 Adams St., Denver, CO 80206; 303/814-0713;
kathy@archstyle.net
Contractor: Bob Nettleton, Nicholas Custom Homes,
Inc.; 4750 S. Santa Fe Cir., Unit #7, Englewood, CO
80110; 303/660-4467; nchinc@aol.com
Furniture builder: Paul Bruning, Bruning's Custom
Woodworking, LLC; 5800 E. 58th Ave., #K, Commerce
City, CO 80022; 303/667-4312
Trim carpenter: Jordon Ishii, Aztec Divide Interiors;
6547 Nile Circle, Arvada, CO 80007; 720/641-5912;
adicustom@hotmail.com
Metalsmith: McSwain Metal Fabrication; 2800 S. Vallejo
St., Englewood, CO 80110; 303/781-1827
Wine room storage: Apex Wine Cellars; 12448 Dumont
Way Littleton, Colorado 80125; 720/733-9026;
brianw@groupapex.com; www.apexwinecellars.com
Kitchen stools: Roche Bobois; 8330 S. Colorado Blvd.,
Littleton, CO 80126; 303/721-1616
Kitchen cabinets: Irpinia Kitchens; 250 Steele St.,
Denver, CO 80206; 720/941-7006; www.irpinia.com

Pages 19, 25, 49 (bottom), 55, 118, 136 (top), 138, 163 (right)
Field editor: Elaine St. Louis
Photographer: Emily Minton Redfield
Architect: J. Mark Nelson; 1815 N. Nevada Ave.,

Colorado Springs, CO 80907; 719/578-9289;
www.jmarknelson.com
Contractor: Blue Sky Construction; 6320 Burgess Rd.,
Colorado Springs, CO 80908; 719/495-2946
Designer: Karen Jones, Decorating on a Dime; 701
County Rd., Palmer Lake, CO 80133; 719/559-1220;
decondime@aol.com
Woodworker: Randy Hall, Hall Woodworks;
2155 Reliable Cir., Colorado Springs, CO 80906
719/471-7449; randyh@hallwoodworks.com
Kitchen cabinets: Monte L. Gagg, Artisan Kitchen
Designs; 1763 S. Eighth St., #4, Colorado Springs, CO
80906; 719/632-2224; www.artisankitchendesigns.com
Entertainment center: Rick Carlson, Carlson
Woodworking; P.O. Box 157, Peyton, CO 80831;
719/749-2508

Pages 16, 108 (bottom), 190
Field editor: Karin Lidbeck-Brent
Photographer: Jim Westphalen
Designers: Milford Cushman, principal, and Chad
Forcier, project designer, The Cushman Design Group,
Inc.; P.O. Box 655, 100 Mountain Road Stowe, VT
05672; 802/253-2169; info@cushmandesign.com;
www.cushmandesign.com
Contractor: Alec Genung Construction, Inc.; P.O. Box
3254 Stowe, VT 05672; 802/793-6284; alec@pshift.com
Interior designer: Rebekah L. Bose, project manager,
and Kim Deetjen, designer, Truex Cullins & Partners
Interiors; 209 Battery St., Burlington, VT 05401;
802/658-2775; www.truexcullins.com

Pages 120
Field editor: Elaine St. Louis
Photographer: Tim Murphy
Builder: Classic Homeworks; 281 S. Pearl St., Denver,
CO 80209; 303/722-3000; info@classichomeworks.com

**Pages 54 (right), 60, 61, 75, 123 (left), 126, 129, 134
(bottom), 142, 149,
 167, 207**
Field editor: Leigh Elmore
Photographer: Kim Golding

Pages 194–199
Interior designer: Patricia Gaylor, Patricia Gaylor
Interior Design; www.patriciagaylor.com

GLOSSARY

Accent lighting. A beam of light three to five times brighter than general lighting that typically is used to highlight a focal point in a room.

Ambient lighting. General overhead lighting that illuminates an entire room.

Balusters. Spindles that help support a staircase handrail.

Batten. A narrow strip used to cover joints between boards and panels.

Beam. A horizontal support member. *See also* Post and Post-and-beam.

Bearing wall. An interior or exterior wall that helps support the roof or the floor joints above.

Board. A piece of lumber that is less than 2 inches thick and more than 3 inches wide.

Board foot. The standard unit of measurement for wood. One board foot is equal to a piece 12×12×1 inches (nominal size).

Building codes. Community ordinances governing the manner in which a home or other structure may be constructed or modified. Most codes deal primarily with fire and health concerns and have separate sections relating to electrical, plumbing, and structural work. *See also* Zoning.

Butt. To place materials end-to-end or end-to-edge without overlapping.

Cantilever. A beam or beams projecting beyond a support member.

...ng. Trimming around a door, window, or other

Cement. A powder that serves as the binding element in concrete and mortar. Also, any adhesive.

Chroma. A hue's brightness or dullness.

Codes. *See* Building codes.

Concrete. A basic building and paving material made by mixing water with sand, gravel, and cement. *See also* Mortar *and* Cement.

Cornice. Any molding or group of molding used in the corner between a wall and ceiling.

Dehumidifier. A device that removes moisture from the air.

Dewatering system. An interior drainage system, such as a dehumidifier or sump pump, meant to keep a basement dry.

Dimmer. A control that offers easy adjustment of lighting levels.

Downlight. A spotlight, either recessed or attached to the ceiling, that directs light downward.

Downspout. A pipe used to drain rainwater from the roof.

Drapery. A decorative window treatment used to control privacy and block light.

Drywall. An interior building material consisting of sheets of gypsum that are faced with heavy paper on both sides. Also known as gypsum board or plasterboard.

Egress. A window that provides an easily accessible opening for escape during an emergency such as a fire.

Flue. A pipe or other channel that carries smoke and combustion gases to the outside air.

Footing. The base on which a masonry wall rests. It spreads the load.

Foundation wall. A bearing perimeter wall, often made of poured concrete, that encloses a full basement.

Framing. The skeletal or structural support of a home, which is sometimes called framework.

Furring. Lightweight wood or metal strips that even a wall or ceiling for paneling. On masonry, furring provides a surface on which to nail.

General-purpose circuit. An electrical circuit that serves several light and/or receptacle outlets. *See also* Heavy-duty circuit.

Grade. Ground level. Also, the elevation at any given point.

Ground fault circuit interrupter (GFCI). A safety device that senses any shock hazard and shuts down a circuit or receptacle.

Hardboard. A manufactured building material made by pressing wood fibers into sheet goods.

Hardwood. Lumber derived from deciduous trees such as oaks, maples, and walnuts.

Header. The framing component spanning a door or window opening in a wall. A header supports the weight above it and serves as a nailing surface for the door or window frame. In masonry, a header course of bricks or stones laid on edge provides strength.

Headroom. Vertical space below the ceiling that allows for standing or moving.

Heat gain. Heat coming into a home from sources other than its heating/cooling system. Most gains come from the sun.

Heat loss. Heat escaping from a home. Heat gains and losses are expressed in Btu per hour.

Heavy-duty circuit. An electrical circuit serving one 120- to 240-volt appliance. *See* General-purpose circuit.

Hue. Another word for color, most often used to identify a specific color.

Jamb. The top and side frames of a door or window opening.

Joint compound. A synthetic-base premixed paste used in combination with paper or fiberglass tape to conceal joints between drywall panels.

Joists. Horizontal framing members that support a floor and/or ceiling.

Laminate. A hard plastic decorative veneer applied to cabinets and shelves.

Level. True horizontal. Also a tool used to determine level. *See* Plumb.

Linear foot. A term used to refer to the length of a board or piece of molding, as opposed to board foot.

Lintel. A load-bearing beam over an opening, such as a door or fireplace, in masonry.

Molding. A strip of wood, usually small-dimensioned, used to cover exposed edges or as decoration.

Mortar. The bonding agent between bricks, blocks, or other masonry units. Consists of water, sand, and cement, but not gravel. *See* Concrete.

Newel post. A post at the bottom, landing, or top of a staircase to which the handrail is secured.

Panel. Wood, glass, plastic, or other material set into a frame, such as in a door. Also, a large, flat, rectangular building material such as plywood, hardboard, or drywall.

Particleboard. Panels made from compressed wood chips and glue.

Partition. An interior dividing wall that may be bearing.

Plywood. A material made of sheets of wood glued or cemented together.

Post. Any vertical support member.

Post-and-beam. A basic building method that uses a few hefty posts and beams to support an entire structure. Contrasts with stud framing.

Pressure-treated wood. Lumber and sheet goods impregnated with one of several solutions to make the wood more impervious to moisture and weather.

~lvvinyl chloride). A type of plastic pipe that's or cold water, but not hot.

Radiant-heat flooring. A heating system installed between the subfloor and the finish floor using a network of electrical heating cables or tubes to hold hot water.

Retaining wall. A structure that holds back a slope and prevents erosion.

Riser. The upright piece between two stairsteps.

Roughing in. The initial stage of a plumbing, electrical, carpentry, or other project, when all components that won't be seen after the second finishing phase are assembled. Also, the framing stage of a carpentry project. This framework later is concealed in the finishing stages.

R-value. A measure of the resistance to heat transfer that an insulating material offers. The higher the R-value, the more effective the insulation.

Sash. The part of a window that can be opened, consisting of a frame and one or more panes of glass.

Sealer. A protective, usually clear, coating applied to wood or metal.

Sill. The lowest horizontal piece of a window, door, or wall framework.

Softwood. Lumber derived from coniferous trees such as pines, firs, cedars, or redwoods.

Stud framing. A building method that distributes structural loads to each of a series of relatively lightweight studs. Contrasts with post-and-beam.

Studs. Vertical 2×3, 2×4, or 2×6 framing members spaced at regular intervals within a wall.

Subfloor. The first layer of a floor. Usually made with planks laid across joists.

Sump pump. A drainage system that pumps and lifts water from a basement to an outside trench or drain.

Suspended ceiling. A low-cost, low-maintenance ceiling option consisting of lightweight acoustical panels supported by a framework of metal channels hung on joist-attached wires. Also referred to as a drop ceiling.

Task lighting. A layer of lighting targeted at specific work areas meant to illuminate and eliminate shadows.

Tint. The result when white is added to a color.

Tone. A color's intensity or degree of lightness or darkness.

Track lights. A versatile lighting fixture consisting of lights on a track that swivel and shift, providing general, task, or accent lighting.

Tread. The level part of a staircase. *See also* Riser.

Threshold. The plate at the bottom of some—usually exterior—door openings. Sometimes called a saddle.

Underlayment. Cementlike product that is used to level floors prior to laying the surface material. Sometimes used to refer to the subfloor material or material laid on top of the subfloor. Usually some type of plywood installed below the surface material of the floor. *See also* Subfloor.

Universal design. The design of products or environments that allows accessibility to all people, regardless of age or ability.

Uplights. Fixtures that direct light toward the ceiling.

U-value. The amount of heat that is allowed to flow through a window.

Valance. Decorative curtain used to conceal the mounting hardware at the top of curtain fixtures.

Vapor barrier. A waterproof membrane in a floor, wall, or ceiling that blocks the transfer of condensation.

Veneer. A thin layer of decorative wood laminated to the surface of a more common wood.

Wainscoting. Any trim or decorative finish along the lower portion of a wall.

Water table. Naturally occurring water that flows through soil like an underground river.

Window well. The open space between a below-grade window and the soil, commonly retained by a steel insert, which allows light to enter the basement.

Zoning. Ordinances regulating the ways in which a property may be used in a given neighborhood. Zoning laws may limit where you can locate a structure.

INDEX

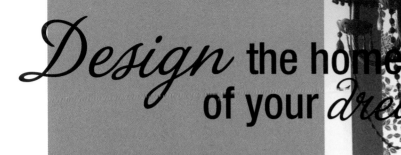

Design the home of your *dreams*

Do it all, your way!

Express yourself with a customized home to fit your style. Give any room personality with decorating ideas, paint techniques, design tips, and how-to instruction that can be found in these inspiring books.

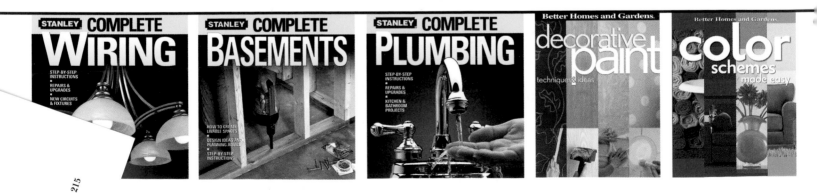

215

dith
O K S

Available where all quality books are sold.